ERO

EROTIC ORIENTATION:
Helping Couples and Individuals Understand Their Sexual Lives

By Joe Kort, Ph.D., LMSW, CST

Smart Sex - Smart Love Books
Royal Oak, Michigan

EROTIC ORIENTATION

Notice to Readers

This book is intended as a reference volume only. It is not a medical manual. The information contained in this book was written to help readers make informed decisions about their sexual practices and about health issues associated with sexuality. It was not designed as a substitute for any treatment that may have been prescribed by your personal physician. If you suspect that you have a medical problem, see a competent physician to discuss your concerns.

This book is also meant to be a short and quick read on topics that so many couples who arrive in my office are struggling with. In the future it may become a larger book with more information and case examples. The intention of this book is to introduce readers to the typical issues couples face over time in relationships, whether they are a straight, gay or mixed-orientation couple.

© Copyright 2019 by Joe Kort, Ph.D.

All rights reserved. No portion of this book may be reproduced in any form without written permission of the author.

EROTIC ORIENTATION

TABLE OF CONTENTS

Introduction. The Trouble with Sex	1
Chapter 1. Healthy Sexuality	6
Chapter 2. Erotic Orientation vs Sexual Orientation	9
Chapter 3. What About Cheating?	15
Chapter 4. Pornography	20
Chapter 5. The Big Taboo: Masturbation	33
Chapter 6. Monogamy, Polyamory, and Open Relationships	38
Chapter 7. Emotional Landscape and Attachment	46
Chapter 8. Sexual Fantasies and Integrity/Erotic Intelligence	50
Chapter 9. Sexual Intimacy and Erotic Differences	60
Chapter 10. Problematic Sexual Behaviors	71
Conclusion	83

INTRODUCTION: THE TROUBLE WITH SEX

In a therapist's office the client says, "There are things I keep hidden from you, Dr. Floyd," and the therapist responds, "And I want you to know how much I appreciate that, Mr. Pendleton."

— J.C. Duffy, Cartoonist

    We live in a world that is deeply confused and conflicted about all matters sexual. If we talk about it at all it is often in whispers, "dirty" talk, or from a negative perspective such as sexual abuse, sexual trauma, or negative and incorrect messages we heard during our formative years.

    Even therapists are uncomfortable talking to their clients about sexuality as depicted in the comic quote above by the late syndicated cartoonist J.C. Duffy (he wrote the Fusco Brothers series and cartoons for the *New Yorker*).

    Unfortunately, most therapists feel like Dr. Floyd when it comes to their clients' sexual confessions. They are not trained in working with the amazing range of sexual expression that exists within each person, nor for approaching the subject in a sex-positive way—that is, as healthy sexuality, not pathological behavior. Fortunately, there are a growing number of therapists delving into this rich and largely taboo subject, such as couples' therapist, author and popular speaker Esther Perel (*The State of Affairs: Rethinking Infidelity*, and *Mating in Captivity: Unlocking Erotic Intelligence*, to name just a few titles). The American Society of Sex Educators, Counselors and Therapists

EROTIC ORIENTATION

(AASECT) of which I am a certified sex therapist and supervisor, certifies sex therapists and does great work in this area, as well, and an increasing amount of literature is coming from a sex-positive place. We are all still pioneering this path and have a long way to go.

As a trained sex therapist, I give talks to groups of other therapists around the country and internationally, and I often ask for a show of hands of those who have had any kind of sex-therapy training, even a one-day workshop. In a roomful of 50 or 60 therapists, I usually get no more than three or four hands. If I give a talk on problematic sexual behaviors, marital therapy, or sexual trauma and abuse, I fill a room. If I offer a talk on helping individuals and couples with sexual pleasure, less than half as many people will show up.

It is troubling that in a profession seeking to help people in their relationships and personal struggles, such a fundamental element as sexual and erotic intimacy is either avoided or not deeply studied by therapists. During therapy, when sexual issues arise, most therapists will often fall back on their training about sexual trauma, sexual abuse, and problematic sexual behaviors, seeking out these dark pathologies in order to deal with them. Sex therapists also rule out pathology around sexual behaviors, but they do so from an informed sexual health and sex-positivity framework. Too often, the untrained therapist makes unsound judgments about what constitutes a healthy sex life—perhaps based their own sexual history of abuse or trauma or infidelity—project this onto the clients and then lead the individual or couple, accordingly, often taking sides with the person who feels aggrieved in the relationship. This is not helpful.

Another problem arises in a term that is far too often used in popular and therapeutic language: "sex addiction." A fight has been going on for years between those who ascribe to the notion that people struggling with "out of control" sexual behaviors should be labeled "sex addicts" (and treated under the same protocols as other types of addicts), and those who believe such people must be understood and treated in a more psychotherapeutic way—one that is more sexually informed. Recently the ICD-11 (the International Classification of Disease, used as a coding manual in healthcare for mental health diagnosis), which therapists use for diagnosis and assessment, included a diagnosis called "Compulsive Sexual Behavior Disorder." This is not "sexual addiction" but rather is listed under the grouping of impulse disorders not addictive or substance disorders.

In my view, and from my years of experience as a sex therapist, the label "sex addiction" is outdated, and should be relegated to history. A more nuanced and realistic view of sexual behavior, one that is not subject to society's archaic and negative attitudes about sex and focuses instead on sex-positive attitudes and a deeper understanding of what sexual health is.

In other words, what about pleasure and fun this most universal of human activities? When we begin to study healthy sex, we are suddenly presented with myriad worlds of sexual desires and practices that are quite normal, even healthy, for a particular client and couple. While before we may have been successful helping someone deal with sexual abuse issues, we have not helped the individual or couple into a conversation about sexual health including sexual pleasure, or their sexual differences.

Sex therapy: What it is, and what it isn't

Recently I had an experience while in the process of moving my office to a new location. My practice operates under the name, "The Center for Relationship and Sexual Health." But when the name was listed on the building directory, I got a call from the building's owner. "We want to have a neutral building that doesn't have any words that are upsetting to people," he said. A pediatrician in the building had filed a complaint, concerned that her clients—parents and children—who saw the sign would be offended and take their business elsewhere. The owner asked others what they thought "sexual health" implied, and he reported that most thought it meant there would be *sexual offenders* in the building. It never occurred to me that these two words could be so widely misconstrued.

In some ways, I shouldn't have been surprised. Despite the fact that we are living at a time in which the words "sex" and "sexual" are daily in the public forum—nearly all in the negative context of harassment and assault (#MeToo; #TimesUp; a President who brags about sexually assaulting women; politicians, pastors, and priests preying upon minors), the word "sex" retains a sort of taboo in the public forum, and people regularly project their own negative connotations onto it. At times when I have mentioned "sexual health" in conversations, I have been asked, "Are you having sex with your clients?" Or, "Is sex therapy just supporting the idea that 'anything goes?'" We are even sometimes confused with sexual surrogates.

None of this is part of sex therapy or sexual health.

To set the record straight, sexual-health therapy is "talk therapy," not having sex in the office, and deals with such things as:

- helping couples with discrepancies in their erotic desires and fantasies
- problems related to painful intercourse or erectile disorders
- sexual difficulties following cancer treatment or childbirth
- breaking of relationship contracts and infidelity
- problems underlying the cessation of sex in a relationship
- religion-based shame around sexuality
- fighting over the use of porn by one or the other partner
- failure to have an orgasm

- helping parents to have conversations with their children or teenagers about sex

Couples and sex therapy

Couples come to therapy to deal with problems in their relationship, but they usually have problems in their sexual side of their relationship, as well. So there needs to be two separate, parallel conversations, one about the emotional health within relationships and the other about sexual health within the relationship. Many people think that if the relationship gets better, then the sex will get better as well, or vice versa. Both are a myth.

Working with couples it is important to encourage them to speak openly about their erotic desires and fantasies, something that seldom happens outside of the therapist's office unless their sexual behaviors and fantasies are interfering with their lives. When these are brought out into the open, they often discover a big discrepancy between each other's inner erotic worlds. Exploring such uncomfortable desires more deeply can open a door to greater understanding of themselves, increased empathy for their partners, and potentially lead to healing their sex lives and their relationship.

So, what I want to do here is to begin to familiarize you with some of the remarkable nuances of human sexual expression, and my attitude toward these. I will address what healthy sexuality is, erotic differences between couples, and issues of infidelity, porn use, masturbation, monogamy, attachment, sexual fantasies and their meaning, and more.

In doing so the hope is that some of the shame and misconceptions surrounding sexuality may be banished, and we can begin to have more adult conversations and understanding of the forces and experiences that lie at the base of our expressions of intimacy.

1 HEALTHY SEXUALITY

Before we explore sexual and erotic orientation, we need to understand healthy versus unhealthy sexuality. In their book *Treating Out of Control Sexual Behavior: Rethinking Sex Addiction*, sex therapists Doug Braun-Harvey and Michael Vigorito provide the best description I've encountered of what is involved in the dimensions of healthy sexuality. They describe *six principles* to recognize if your sexual behaviors are healthy or not:

1. Consent
2. Non-exploitive
3. Safer Sex
4. Honesty
5. Shared Values
6. Mutually Pleasurable

While many of these principles are self-explanatory, let's unpack consent. Consent is black and white: before sexual behavior begins, all parties involved must verbally agree to the behavior, consent can be revoked at any moment for any reason, and that sexual behavior must stop.

Since we will be digging deeper into sexual behaviors such as role-playing and kinks that can come with a risk or personal safety if not performed correctly, let's define consent a little further and its cousin, consensual non-consent.

Before starting sexual play that is exploratory or risky, all parties involved should have a conversation and agreement about what each partner will be doing, and a code word that if any partner uses, brings that sexual play to an immediate end.

In contrast, "consensual non-consent," a particular type of kink, does not always have a code word. Beforehand, each person talks about what they want to do, and sexual play only begins when everyone has agreed. This requires a lot of trust. Everyone involved should have several conversations, clear understanding and agreement that once play starts, each partner can do what they want and do not necessarily have to stop, even when they are told to. This idea of going to the edge—and the possibility of going over it—is very erotic for some individuals. Of course, in reality if the submissive wants to stop all play will end, but there is an enjoyment of the inclusion of non-consent.

If a partner asks you to consider consensual non-consent sexual activity, before agreeing to this you should evaluate your erotic orientation and consider having conversations about it. I would caution anyone who has a history of abuse, neglect, or any other kind of trauma to be extremely careful with this type of sexual activity. Agreeing to non-consent sexual play could put you at risk for triggering your trauma and having a negative outcome. On the other hand, if you have had trauma and accept the possibility of triggers, it might be erotic for you to go to the edge without being able to say no where you might experience real surrender.

There are, of course, ethical limits to kinky sexual activity that should be considered before beginning. For example, I had a client who was into knife play. In the midst of sexual activity, the woman began using a knife on his back—not a fixed, dull blade like they had agreed to, but a serrated blade. Because it didn't feel right, he immediately asked her to stop and discovered he was bleeding. They had never negotiated for anything other than a dull blade, and she

EROTIC ORIENTATION

did not ask permission to use the knife she chose. Now he has a scar all the way down his back. She stopped when he asked her to and helped him clean up the cuts, but what she did was not consensual and should not have occurred.

As you read on, consider whether your erotic orientation (sexual desires, fantasies, and behaviors) has these healthy principles. If not, I suggest seeking out a therapist who understands how to help you understand them. If you're acting out any fantasy that puts you or others at risk in any way, you should seek help immediately.

Jack Morin, author of *The Erotic Mind: Unlocking the Inner Sources of Sexual Passion and Fulfillment*, invites people to explore their peak sexual experiences, favorite masturbation fantasies, and the pornography they choose to read and watch. He argues that examining these things helps you to discern your core erotic theme (CET). This internal blueprint for arousal, Morin says, "transforms old wounds and conflicts into excitation." He goes on to say that "hidden in within your CET is a formula for transforming unfinished emotional business from childhood and adolescence into excitation and pleasure."

Unless their sexual behaviors and fantasies are interfering with their lives most people don't consider examining them. In my therapy practice, however, I find some clients are suffering from behaviors and desires they don't like and wish they did not have (you will find such examples throughout this book). Usually this comes from guilt and shame instilled in them from their religious upbringing or cultural expectations. However, even for these folks, exploring such uncomfortable desires more deeply can open a door to greater understanding of themselves.

In other words, everyone can learn more about themselves from their sexual behaviors and fantasies. So, let's explore this concept of erotic orientation, and how it differs from sexual orientation.

2 EROTIC ORIENTATION VS. SEXUAL ORIENTATION

Our erotic orientation—our behaviors, fantasies, and preferences—do not always match up with the society's (or our own) expectations about someone's sexual orientation. For example, some gay men fantasize about women, some lesbians fantasize about men, some straight men imagine themselves giving a blowjob to a disembodied penis and some straight women eroticize being with other women. Many gay men fantasize about having sex with straight men and many women fantasize about being sexual with gay men. There is an increasing amount of gay men interested in being sexual with transgender men who have not had bottom surgery. These gay men are attracted to the masculinity of the transgender men while enjoying PIV (penis in vagina) sex. This is no different from straight men enjoying sexual contact with transgender women who have not had bottom surgery. These men talk about attraction to women with, "watermelon breasts, painted fingernails, full makeup and colored hair," allowing the man to visually experience a woman, but with the addition of a penis and testicles. This gives men the opportunity to experience aspects of gay sex while still being with a woman.

It can be a part of someone's erotic orientation to have desires for someone that cannot be fulfilled or would be seen as deviating from their sexual orientation. Our erotic orientation does not always match up with the society's (or our own) expectations about our own or someone else's sexual orientation.

Being caught up in a moment, in a certain situation, wanting to get off, or merely wanting to experiment are just some of the reasons why sexuality is fluid and not bound by strict rules.

As an example, I once worked with a lesbian who was left by several girlfriends because she fantasized about being gang-raped by men. This woman was not bothered by her sexual and erotic interest in this fantasy, nor had she ever had it happen, nor was she going to make it happen. For her it didn't matter where the fantasy came from or that it was politically against her core beliefs. It was just a fantasy. Sadly, that was not how a few of her girlfriends saw this. The decision going forward was to be wary about telling any future partners and perhaps not telling them at all.

Straight men and women also might fantasize about being intimate with or even engaging in sexual behavior with someone of the same sex without it affecting their sexual or romantic orientation. Being caught up in a moment, in a certain situation, wanting to get off, or merely wanting to experiment are just some of the reasons why sexuality is fluid and not bound by strict rules.

Essentially, you aren't what you orgasm

In *Arousal*, Michael Bader describes straight women being sexually attracted to gay men because they're "safe." He writes that these women can become "sexually expressive in a more confident and spontaneous way than they can with straight men because their overtures will not be reciprocated. These are women who have anxieties about being sexual with straight men because they're "afraid of being overpowered or rejected." A gay man usually won't cross the line toward her, making it safe for women to flirt and be sexually aggressive with him without risking rejection. If she convinces the gay guy to be sexual with her, Bader says, this is "reassurance that she is *especially* attractive."

I've also heard countless gay male clients tell me of their interest in "getting sexual with a straight man" for one night. Some clients talk about wanting to "service" him without reciprocation. Others want him to participate by talking or telling him what to do, while still others want him to lay back and be worshiped. Whatever the case, it gives the gay man more information about himself once he cracks the erotic code and understands, as there are nonsexual narratives behind each one of these scenarios.

For instance, sexual fantasies gay men have about straight men are sometimes longings for acceptance by straight men in general or by their father. Straight men can be stand-ins for father figures. Gay men hear over and over that such men would never accept a "fem boy"—which many of them have accepted that they are simply for being gay. Because of this, some gay men often fear straight men. As children, they love these male figures and want their acceptance; as adults, they sexualize these straight men because it unconsciously offers a way to feel safely and pleasantly attached to them. In the sexual fantasy of pleasing a straight guy, you finally get a chance to make contact with him and get the approval you have always wanted.

Sexual orientation is a constant

It does not change. This can be confusing when someone owns up to their true inner desires that involve someone of a different sex to which they are attracted. For example, it looks as though the person changes from gay to straight orientation when in fact they are becoming who they really are. They stop role-playing the wrong orientation and come out of denial as to who they truly are.

Heterosexual men enjoy the company of women, romantically and sexually. They are aroused and feel compelled to have sex with women. However, when they're in prison or in the armed forces where women are not available, often they will find sexual gratification with other men. This doesn't mean that they have switched to a gay or bisexual orientation or even sexually fluid, but simply they have no one but other men available for sexual release. Once these heterosexual men get released or discharged, back they go to their female objects of desire and usually never again have sex with men.

Conversely, heterosexually married gay men have often fallen in love with their wives and been sexual with them. They're often monogamous, performing sexually and enjoying orgasms with these women, and are sexually satisfied. They are not bisexual; nor are they heterosexual men gone bad! They have either chosen—or felt compelled—to live heterosexually but are innately gay. In some ways this is a personal prison imposed upon one's self by not permitting their homosexuality to come out. Once divorced, they seek out other men exclusively for sexual gratification, and never do return to women.

Influences from childhood

One's love map and sexual preference map is determined early in childhood. Who we fall in love with and what turns us on sexually is our romantic and sexual preference. It is how we learn how to love. We observe and absorb how others love or neglect or abuse us and that becomes our "love map," according to John Money, a pioneer in the field of sexology. This map becomes a template for what you seek out for pleasure in your adulthood. This is different from sexual orientation where we have science pointing us in the direction that one is "born that way" and cannot be shaped into any sexual orientation.

As children, we're all imprinted with family beliefs and societal norms. Imprinting is the psychological process by which specific types of behavior are locked in at an early stage of development. All of us are conditioned to think, feel, and act the way our early childhood caretakers nurture and teach us.

Consider the boy who was sexually abused by an adult man. Later he might engage in what we call *trauma reenactment* with other men sexually by seeking out homosexual sexual acts. This doesn't make him gay or even bisexual. He is simply left with an imprint to behaviorally re-enact his homosexual abuse and may later find erotic "pleasure" in what was inflicted on him as a child. In reality, this isn't pleasure at all, but trauma turned into orgasm. John M. Preble and A. Nicholas Groth say it best in their book, *Male Victims of Same-Sex Abuse: Addressing Their Sexual Response.* "…this may actually reflect an effort at mastery of the traumatic event …when he was being sexually victimized, someone else was in control of him sexually. During masturbation he is literally in control of himself sexually, and this may be a way in which he attempts to reclaim mastery over his own sexuality. Likewise, his participation in consensual sex reflects his choice and decision."

The authors go on to say that "…fantasy thoughts are prompted by fear more than desire, by anxiety more than pleasure." In other words, they become a way of managing fear and anxiety.

Many males who are sexually abused by male perpetrators as children believe it was something "gay" that happened to them. But when men sexually abuse girls, we don't claim it's about heterosexuality! We say it is simply sexual abuse, which involves power, violation and rape. Nothing about that is related to orientation.

Homoeroticism

This is the concept that men and women (who are basically heterosexual, of course) can enjoy some sexual activity with members of their own gender—if only vicariously. Surfing the Internet, you can find thousands of sites with tag lines like:

"Do my wife while I watch"

EROTIC ORIENTATION

"My husband is too small—I need to show him something bigger"

"My wife wants a female partner to join in with us"

"Voyeur to watch you and your spouse"

Such preferences don't necessarily imply sexual abuse or homosexual imprinting, nor do they necessarily involve bisexuality or homosexuality. There are simply men and women who, from time to time, become aroused by the same gender enjoying sexual activity with them. Indeed, research has shown that some men and women are even turned on by the idea of their spouses having an affair. For them, there is something homoerotic in the idea, just as in "swinging," when couples enjoy bringing in others to be sexual with them, temporarily, without breaking up their committed relationship (more on this in a later chapter). However, they may not admit to homosexual desire. In his book, *Extramarital Affair*, Herbert S. Strean writes, "Couples who openly advocate extramarital affairs also derive a great deal of pleasure [because] they identify with their spouse and unconsciously have sex with [their] spouse's lover." Strean says, "Because this is unconscious process, most couples who sanction extramarital activity deny their homosexual involvement and justify their stance on the basis of free expression."

3 WHAT ABOUT CHEATING?

Infidelity is one of the top reasons couples come to me for counseling.

They are desperate to stay together and want sincerely to work through the pain and betrayal. Infidelity can hurt nearly as much as the pain we experience when someone we know has been murdered. In reality, the old marriage *has* died. But that doesn't mean that there can't be a *new* marriage. I'm happy to say, in fact, that it *is* possible—and I can testify to the fact that, if a relationship can survive an affair and get to the other side of healing, it becomes better than ever. It doesn't happen, though, without a lot of hard work and difficult conversation.

The reason it gets better? Because most couples have not had the harder sexual and erotic conversations that would make it possible to avoid affairs.

To avoid having those conversations people "act out" their fantasies and sexual desires and even romantic desires with someone for whom it won't matter if they are judged or criticized. It is harder to have core talks with partners about our deepest and darkest desires and interests, and so much easier with a stranger. Once an affair is exposed, if the couple is willing to do the hard work and talk about those core desires that should have been talked about all along, then I have seen the relationship strengthen and the bond with one another become tighter.

Some researchers have estimated that marital infidelity occurs in about 2.3 percent of married women, and about 4.3 percent of married men. Other studies suggest that as many as 25 percent of men and 11 percent of women will, at some point in their lives, end up in bed with someone other than their partner. I suspect the numbers are even higher.

One of the most common and difficult things to work through after infidelity is seeing the relationship in terms of perpetrator and victim. Love and desire are extremely subtle and complicated emotions. Esther Perel, the internationally known author and psychotherapist specializing in infidelity, says, "The dilemmas of love and desire are way too complex to yield simple answers of good and bad, victim and perpetrator, right and wrong."

I agree.

It makes sense in the beginning that the betrayed partner feels—and is—victimized by infidelity. One man said in my office, "I have been in an open marriage for 20 years and didn't even know it." However, if the betrayed partner, for example, takes the victim's attitude for a prolonged period of time and says, "You did this to me, and now it is up to you to fix this problem, because I have nothing to do with it," then the problem will neither be understood nor resolved. The partner who broke the relationship contract may have personal reasons within themselves for why they went outside the relationship.

The problem contributing to infidelity can have its root in sexual frustration, feeling neglected or neglecting, feeling ignored or ignoring, loneliness, or many other things. Condemnation and taking refuge in the role of victim is useless. Even worse is when the injured party becomes the *shamed* one, as in when a friend or relative says, "How could you even *think* of staying with that cheater after what he did to you?" It takes real courage to face the subtle problems in a relationship that have led to infidelity. Such simple judgments by others only compound the problem. At the same time, the involved partner must be willing to talk about it openly, and way beyond his or her comfort level. The involved partner has to be willing to listen to the pain of the injured partner for as long as is needed to begin to lessen the trauma and emotions around the infidelity, and to begin to rebuild trust. They must be able and willing to feel and share their remorse, guilt, and empathy for the hurt they caused.

At the same time, the injured partner may be able to discover something in his or her behavior that contributed to the infidelity. I'll share one example of how this worked.

A couple came to me after the woman discovered that the man had been carrying on a two-year affair with a woman half his age. As we delved into his infidelity, he revealed that he really had no interest in a real or lasting relationship with the other woman. He simply objectified her as someone who was willing to enact the erotic fantasies he'd harbored for years. When he had implied or suggested these to his wife, she had met them with such disgust that he felt ashamed and never again brought them up.

While in therapy, however, his devoutly religious wife said, "You're wrong. I would do anything like that for you. My Bible tells me that you are my husband and we should be able to do whatever we want. I never thought, or realized, that I was shaming you."

Through becoming honest with one another and having a willingness to bridge their erotic and cultural differences, this couple saved their marriage. I believe we can salvage many others if we are willing to challenge the silence and taboos that have pathologized too many of our normal desires.

Here are some other important things I've learned about getting through infidelity to a better place:

Affairs don't necessarily indicate a bad marriage. People cheat for myriad reasons. Some of my clients have told me they cheated because they were too afraid or ashamed to talk to their partner about their sexual preferences or fantasies. They may have cautiously suggested a sexual practice that was met with disbelief, disgust, or accusations of perversion, and vowed never again to raise the subject. However, suppression of a fantasy or desire, as the majority of therapists will acknowledge, does not *rid* a person of the desire. In most cases it simply shoves it into the unconscious where it will eventually come out in inopportune, inappropriate, and destructive ways.

Some men, rather than bringing up such a subject, feel shame. They automatically assume their wife will freak out. They then project their own shame upon their partner, often unjustly. Even if the wife initially is not open to such experimentation, the man's desire for it is not likely to go away, and he may seek out a different avenue with which to vent it. Similarly, a husband's unwillingness to be more romantic doesn't mean his wife's desire for it will go away, either.

Use the right language. My approach is to avoid using language such as cheating, victim and cheater. I take this from the work of psychotherapist and sex therapist Barry McCarthy who teaches the language of the injured party, the involved party and calling it a break in the relationship contract. This reduces reactivity and give the relationship and the partners a chance to recover and survive. Using the other language put everyone and the relationship in jeopardy with less chances to heal.

This talk about infidelity must happen in a controlled situation, i.e. in the presence of a therapist, or in some other ritualized and controlled setting or healing space. This venting of one's pain should not be spontaneous or done in public or in front of other family members or children. Such strong reactivity must be contained by both parties to ensure a healthy dialogue. It is much too vulnerable an interaction, and quickly polarizing for those outside of the relationship. Asking for an appointment with a partner to talk about the topic and putting time limits on the conversation are helpful to keeping things contained and effective in communication.

Transparency is vital. If the involved partner wants to salvage the relationship (or, rather, build a new marriage), he or she is going to have to become completely *transparent* for a period of time. That is, no secret passwords for emails or computers, no secret meetings or letters. Nothing can ever be deleted. Privacy is not a priority at this time. If not, the injured partner cannot learn to trust again. Over time, the injured partner needs to understand that total transparency is no longer useful and needs to prepare for that to end and learn to trust in the dark. This is not easy.

I am a couple's therapist. I believe in relationships and marriage. To believe that an injured partner should be shamed for staying and working things out seems to be in conflict with our cultural message that marriage and relationships *matter* and should be fought for. Infidelity has been with us since the institution of marriage began. Therefore, it is important as a society to come to terms with the reality, to find ways to effectively deal with the shame and pain, and to try to help couples reestablish the bonds that brought them together. As for the broader question of monogamy, as a society we may eventually have to come to terms with the idea that some of us are simply not well suited to it.

Problems sometimes arise when a man is caught by his female partner looking at pornography, which the partner views as cheating. I have had women tell me in my office that finding his porn is like finding him in bed with another woman. This is a subtler and often more challenging problem than if his partner had found him in bed with another woman. However, if the couple is willing to talk openly in a therapist's office about this, about their inner fantasies for which porn provides an outlet, a great deal of healing and strengthening of the relationship can happen. Women often take it very personally that their male partner is watching porn, and men often cannot find ways to let women know that the porn is separate from his relationship with her.

So, let's address viewing porn—why it happens and how it can cause problems in a relationship and/or can even be a positive thing.

4 PORNOGRAPHY

"We are not making love; we are making movies."
—Miles Stryker, porn actor

Because of the lack of sex education in schools, kids (and many adults) are learning about sex from easily accessible porn. There has been a big push for years to ban porn from minors, but that doesn't stop them from watching it. A serious issue is created when adults want to ban something and make it all go away so that don't have to ever talk about it. But it is *not going away*. It is fine if your family values are to limit and restrict porn but making it taboo makes young people all the more curious and makes it all the more exciting!

The lack of sex-positive, sexual health conversations has led to porn illiteracy. Adults, as well as teens, get the wrong idea of what sex is or lack the understanding that every partner is different in what they like and are interested in doing sexually. This is a perfect setup for embarrassment and misunderstandings between partners whose idea of a good time could be completely different. Maybe a young woman has been watching dominatrix porn and she catches her boyfriend off guard who is expecting her to want relational sex and isn't ready to be dominated.

Author Marty Klein's words of wisdom regarding how to talk to kids about porn are invaluable. In an article on his blog titled, *"Time to Talk to Your Kids About Porn,"* he highlights some key points:

- Porn is created for entertainment not to portray actual sex
- Porn features unusual "perfect" bodies that you should not compare yourself to
- The people are just actors playing a role like in a movie
- Porn doesn't show everything that sex can be

    I found these points to be particularly helpful when I found my nephews watching porn. Their parents didn't want to talk to them about it, and so I did. I told the boys how the actors have sexual health conversations that the viewer doesn't see, something some porn producers are including in the videos before and after the sexual acts, trying to facilitate more awareness of how partners should interact and provide consent before sex begins. I explained how they shouldn't compare a porn star's penis to their own, or how most vulvas in porn are prosthetic for viewing pleasure, when in fact vulvas come in many shapes, sizes, and colors. "You don't have to talk to me about it," I said, "but I'm worried you're gonna try something in the bedroom that your partner isn't prepared for and you're going to humiliate yourself." This peaked their curiosity and allowed them to be willing to let me talk to them about porn even if it was only for a brief few minutes.

Partners vs porn

    It's a story I've heard many times in my practice. A marriage is going along just fine and then a wife discovers that her husband has been watching Internet porn. This porn typically bears little resemblance to what she and her husband do in bed. Maybe the sex is rougher, kinkier, wilder, or the women in the videos look nothing like her. They are younger or older than she is, thinner or fatter, or dressed in fishnet stockings or bustier. Maybe they say nasty words during the sex, things she would never think of uttering.

She can't understand why her man is not completely satisfied sexually with their relationship and needs to find arousal elsewhere.

And frankly, neither does he.

She feels betrayed, almost as if she had found him in bed with another woman. Then the labels come out—*sex addict, pervert, deviant, liar*—raining down upon the husband like spears. He is embarrassed, filled with shame, and swears he'll never again pursue such fantasies. He promises to stop watching porn or anything else in order to help him escape his wife's pain and ease her heartache, anything that can erase the shame he's feeling from being exposed, and the pain it has caused her. And he really means to keep his promise, but in another week, month, or year, he is drawn back to that irresistible make-believe sexual world.

The first advice I offer is, "Let's slow things down." It is critical that partners lower reactivity when learning about the other's sexual interest. Discoveries like this raise hackles that couples didn't even know they had. There are so many unspoken cultural prohibitions and minefields they are going to have to navigate, and it must be done carefully and at least somewhat dispassionately.

So, we must first move the focus away from the porn. Most couples—and too many therapists—focus on the porn as the *problem*. In fact, the porn is often not the problem, but rather each partner's *relationship* to the porn. Too often therapists jump into the conflict, judging the porn and imposing their own beliefs and values onto it (which are often aligned with the wife's). This distracts the couple from getting to the root of the real issue, which is more likely erotic differences.

The question that I ask both partners is, "What is the content of the porn bringing up for each of you?" Both have given the porn a meaning, and I hold the value of that meaning in high regard for both. Her reaction to the porn often points to negative feelings and beliefs she may be carrying about herself. For him, the content of the porn may express parts of himself he may not be able to express nonsexually.

    I help couples by decoding the nonsexual narrative of the porn that they discover. I teach them to see their sexual fantasies as if they are dreams or metaphors. Research indicates that our erotic interests are the result of very early events. For example, a boy growing up with an older sister may sneak a peek at her when she's naked. He may see her pubic hair and find himself attracted throughout his life to unshaved women. Perhaps he saw his mother pulling on a pair of fishnet stockings before she went out, and porn in which women dress this way arouse him forevermore.

Speaking different erotic languages

    Much of the problem lies in the widespread misunderstanding of men's sexuality. Men and women are for the most part living in vastly different erotic worlds, almost as if their erotic self speaks a different language. A woman often wants to hear her husband tell her she's beautiful. She wants him to take her, take all of her. She needs to feel his desire for her, to hear him say, "You're my one and only," or "I love how you make love." Her sexuality is aroused by romance, fed by romantic movies and books. It is relational and thrives on connection.

    Men also seek connection and adoration but often have different language for it. Men can be romantic, but they feel most connected with their partner through sex and much more through their genitals than do women. When a man says, "Take all of me, take me all the way inside you," or "swallow me," he is saying that he wants to deeply feel that connection, to feel how much his manliness is desired. He wants to feel adored and may need to hear from his partner how big or buff he is in her eyes, not necessarily how sweet or romantic he is.

That her man needs to gratify himself with images and fantasies that have nothing to do with her is threatening to his wife, withering even. It brings up all of her own issues around body image, betrayal, self-esteem, and so on. She takes his impersonal act personally:

- Why do you need to see that?
- Why aren't you doing that with me?
- Am I that unattractive?

She feels competitive, but this is *not* a competition. What she doesn't understand is that porn and his feelings for her are apples and oranges, and that it detracts nothing from their relationship. It is neither about the marriage, nor her. Watching porn is such a self-centered activity that he may very well not want to put her in that position, not want to put her into the role of sexual object. Viewed this way, one might even think of it as a considerate, loving thing to exclude her from sexual practices that he believes would offend her!

On the flip side, gay and lesbian couples rarely struggle with porn. This is probably due to the fact that they are comfortable watching it together, not judging the other for admiring the bodies on the screen since they are most likely attracted to the same actors. Sometimes it's not about the actors at all, but the egalitarian aspect of gay porn that draws an audience not only of gay men but also of straight men and women and even lesbians! For example, some lesbians enjoy watching gay male porn together because the power is balanced, both men clearly want to be there, and it is more obvious of mutual enjoyment than straight porn. Lesbians often say that watching "lesbian porn" isn't erotic because most of it is for the enjoyment of a straight man.

Beyond watching and enjoying it together, there are other ways porn can be beneficial in a relationship. If you or your partner have sexual interests that the other is not into (I address this in a later chapter), for some couples, porn can be a way to stay monogamous. By having that outlet, you or your partner can have that sexual fantasy, behavior, or preference satisfied without being physically sexual outside of your relationship.

The tiny-waist couple
A good example of this was a married couple I counseled. The husband's core erotic orientation was towards women with tiny waists. He fell in love with his wife—who had a tiny waist—and they had great sex, even as she had three children and her waist was not as small as it once was. As they aged, they continued to have sexual health conversations and an enjoyable sex life. They came to see me after she found his porn, which was riddled with women who had tiny waists. Her immediate thought was to compare the actors in the videos to herself and the tiny waist she no longer had. "What does this say about me?" she asked.

"Nothing," I told her. "He likes women with tiny waists. That's one reason he met you, fell in love with you, and married you." I asked her if she ever thought he didn't like her body, if she suspected he was thinking of other women while having sex, or if their sex had become more infrequent. To all of this, she replied "no." I helped her to understand that although she had been socialized to compare herself to these women, her marriage was not in danger because he was looking at them in *addition* to her, not instead of. She was enough for him, but he could not deny his core erotic orientation.

Porn can certainly be used "instead of" a partner though. But then it is a relationship or attachment problem, not a porn problem.

I have also seen a similar version of this with women using

their vibrators. Men often come into my office feeling as though their penises have been replaced. "Why does she need that when my dick is available 24/7," they angrily say. As a therapist I would no more blame the vibrator than I would the porn, but rather talk to the man about what it means to him that his wife may want to pleasure herself without him from time to time.

Most couples, if they have chosen monogamy, have not negotiated their relationships. When couples come to see me, I ask them if they have discussed what monogamy means to both of them.

- Can watching porn be okay?
- Does it have to be a certain type of porn?
- Sexting a friend?
- Webcamming with a person in another country with whom you will never meet?
- Can he use a fleshlight?
- Can you flirt and have romantic exchanges that never turn sexual with someone else?

Most heterosexual couples assume they know what it means to be monogamous and that their partner just simply knows. This is dangerous and can lead to problems in the future.

Technology focusing on having sex with others through apps, the internet and devices is everywhere now. A partner can even be lying in bed next to their partner and be engaging in sexual play and talk with someone else unbeknownst to their significant other.

When these things are exposed in the relationship it wreaks havoc for both partners. It is why I urge my clients to talk as openly and honestly about their erotic and sexual needs.

EROTIC ORIENTATION

Cam you see me?

It's been said that the word intimacy breaks down as into me you see. While you can show some of yourself online with a webcam, it's not the same form of intimacy that being face to face demands. Watching our culture—gay, straight, bisexual and across all sexual orientations—become more computer-dependent and using the Internet for more and more contact, some therapists fear that our skills for attachment and intimacy are beginning to atrophy. In many places, people are no longer even going to bars or other social meeting places to find dating partners, but just logging on to the Internet.

Most individuals willing to show themselves on cams are going to be more confident about their looks and their body. For the most part the men will have bigger penises and the women will have larger breasts, and nearly all will have above-average looks. This causes many people to think that their partners should look more like this, causing their sexual attraction to become more narrowly defined.

Some individuals in my office and workshops seem very picky about the type of partner they're looking for and viewing these perfect bodies on a regular basis can add to that pickiness. Straight individuals will be looking for someone with the attractiveness level of an opposite-sex model. Gay and bisexual men and women will compare themselves to same-sex individuals in photos or on webcams and say, "What's wrong with me? I don't look like that! I'll never find a partner!" I tell them that those willing to display themselves are those who have larger endowments or breasts and feel good about their bodies. They're not necessarily people to measure yourself against.

Based on the rising number of live webcam sex sites available on the Internet, both men and women appear to be attracted.

EROTIC ORIENTATION

Sometimes webcam sex serves a positive purpose for many individuals. I have had male clients who have strong fetishes and kinks that they are either too ashamed or worried about the risk of losing a partner to tell them. It is easier for them to get on cam with a complete stranger and engage in live porn. In other words, they are never going to meet this person who often lives very far away. The inter-activeness of the connection helps enhance their sexual desire and orgasm.

Other men do tell their partner, but their partners are either uncomfortable and/or unwilling to engage in certain sexual acts or talks, so they turn to webcam sex to get their needs met.

I have had women tell me that watching porn and using her vibrator is "time for herself." She doesn't want to negotiate with a partner or wait for them to come home. This is her time for herself and doesn't reflect anything about the relationship.

How porn might serve a marriage

Joey and Chrissy were married for ten years and had three children. While they did have conflict from time to time, mostly they were happy—except in the bedroom.

Joey disclosed to me that since the beginning of the marriage he had told Chrissy he needed her to be more engaged in bed by talking more, telling him what to do and initiating some sexual novelty. She would do this for a while, but then go back to her default passive role in the bedroom where Joey would have to be the aggressor and initiator and regularly come up with new things to do. Over the years Joey returned to the conversation asking Chrissy to initiate, be more talkative and lead in the bedroom, but it would go back to old ways.

Joey traveled on a regular basis for work, and during one of his trips he found a website featuring women whom he could pay to cam and with whom he could talk about his fantasies. He tried it and loved it. What he loved were that these women were verbal and brought into the sexual talks new ideas and ways of being turned on. He was unsuccessful getting this with Chrissy, so this became a regular thing for him.

One day he came home to learn that his wife had discovered his webcam sex. She accused him of cheating and called him a "sex addict." In crisis they came into therapy with me. During the session I supported Chrissy's experience of being injured by Joey's use of webcam sex with other women.

"How could you do this to me? To us? Why aren't I enough for you?" she asked.

"You *are* enough for me Chrissy. I prefer to do all of this with you, but I have asked you—it even feels to me like I sometimes begged you—to be more verbal and engaged and lead in our sex life. You would for a brief period and then stop. I grew tired of trying to get you to do something you didn't seem to want to do, like I was pulling you into something that didn't turn you on."

"So, you went to other women behind my back and cheated on me," Chrissy said, crying.

"I don't even know these women!" he said. "Besides they are from Russia. I will never meet them."

"It doesn't matter. You knew better. We were supposed to be monogamous."

Here is where I stepped in as their therapist. Yes, Joey was guilty of secretly doing something Chrissy didn't know about, I said, but they had never negotiated their monogamy contract to include or exclude technology. Is that cheating? If so how and why?

"It's assumed," Chrissy tearfully said.

I said that while it would be nice to assume what monogamy is and is not and get it right with a partner, that isn't how it works. It didn't make Joey's actions right, but I helped her see that this was not something they talked about. I asked her to look at Joey, who now also was crying. "He wants to do this with you in the way that turns him on with you initiating and leading," I said. "I want you to understand that he would let go of all the webcam play if you and he could find a way to get you more active in the bedroom. I want you to take in that he wants you!"

Joey nodded yes to all the things I said.

"I want to do this for you, but it isn't my nature," Chrissy said. "That's why it falls away. I didn't realize how important it was to you." After a pause she said, "Okay, I am willing to try again."

Joey was choked up by that time, and couldn't talk, but he reached out to hold her hand.

Now their relationship had begun to have better communication about both of their erotic needs. It would have been easy for us to focus on Joey breaking the relationship contract by not telling Chrissy he was going to get on webcam with other women to get the erotic needs met he wished she would do. Focusing on the infidelity is easy, but not productive. We also needed to focus on what it meant for Joey to do such a thing. Once we did the healing could begin.

Childhood imprinting

Wayne was CEO of a large company—a stressful position that involved managing many employees. He was a devoted husband and highly responsible man. His wife, Lori, discovered him watching kinky porn—dominatrixes in black leather commanding, gagging, binding and spanking men slaves, belittling them when they failed to precisely follow her instructions, rewarding them when they did. She was appalled to discover that her strong man, this successful leader and father, would harbor such fantasies. He had never suggested to her that they enact such scenes in their sexual lives.

Again, rather than focusing on his porn habit, we explored his childhood. One of four siblings, he'd been brought up in a family that had been erratically managed by a self-absorbed, negligent parent who couldn't be bothered to keep careful track of her children. Early in life, he'd begun to eroticize women who behaved in the opposite way, women who would tell him what to do. This became his core sexual script. In his fantasies, women took charge while he could enjoy being submissive and taking orders. In this fantasy, Wayne unconsciously created the "good parent" who punished when he was bad and rewarded when he was good—something he hadn't had from his parent. My task, then, was to help Wayne and Lori discover how to absorb this new information, define limits with each other, find a way that trust could be restored, and a way they could grow together as a result of the experience. Most often, this kind of exploration opens new feelings of understanding and compassion for each other.

The important thing to remember here, especially if you are freaking out because you found that your partner was watching porn that you had not imagined he or she would be watching, is this: "It's not about you!"

Vive la différence (between men and women)

Generally speaking, and not all that surprisingly, the same stimuli often do not arouse both men and women. When men have fantasies, there is more objectification of the sex partner. Men's fantasies are less about relationship, less about tenderness and dialogue, and more about cutting right to the sexual act. Women's fantasies are more relational, more about romance. They tend to fantasize about love stories, which men seldom do. In general, women more often need to feel partners are courting or seducing them. For men, the gateway to feelings of intimacy is the sex itself. For women, it often is everything leading up to it.

EROTIC ORIENTATION

Why? In our culture, studies show that we stop touching boys around the time they turn eight years old. They receive encouragement, subtly or overtly, to distance themselves from their feelings and to not touch other boys. The outlet for their feelings then often becomes sports, violence, work, and sex. These become the places men have permission to express themselves.

For a girl, on the other hand, touching and expressions of adoration aren't taboo. She may get an erotic buzz when a man tells her how beautiful she looks, or how well she dances. This becomes her template for opening the doors of intimacy in the future. In the popular book, *A Billion Wicked Thoughts*, by neurological researchers Ogi Ogas and Sai Gaddam, we find positive proof. In men, physical arousal and psychological arousal are united, while in women, psychological arousal is separated from physical arousal. The authors describe men's "porntopia" and women's "romantopia."

For couples whose issue is porn, what is often needed is to work on bridging the cultural expectations between the man and the woman. I invite them to begin to talk openly about the differences between their erotic identities without judging the other's as good or bad.

At the very least, this may cultivate some understanding of and compassion for their partner, minimizing the judgment and disgust of the porn they have discovered.

5 THE BIG TABOO: MASTURBATION

It's everyone's dark secret, seldom brought into the light to examine and only talked about as jokes and in whispers.

Mention masturbation aloud in a social setting and watch the reaction, both in listeners and within your own body and mind. It's a loaded subject, fraught with centuries of religious imprecations, misunderstood morality, and guilty self-loathing. Consider this: The reason we have Kellogg's Corn Flakes today is because Dr. John Harvey Kellogg, the Seventh Day Adventist and inventor of the corn flake, called masturbation "self-pollution" and "abominable," and believed eating his corn flakes would reduce one's desire for sex. The minister Sylvester Graham developed Graham crackers for the same reason.

Despite such efforts, masturbation is something that we apparently still have a lot of interest in. A Google search on "masturbation" yields some 94 million choices. One such choice reveals that May has been dubbed "Masturbation Month," something that the purveyor of sex toys, Good Vibrations, began promoting back in the '90s when the then U.S. Surgeon General, Dr. Joycelyn Elders, was brave enough to publicly suggest that children should be taught that masturbation is a natural part of human sexuality, for which she was promptly fired.

Masturbation is *not* unhealthy! In fact, numerous studies show that masturbation has overwhelmingly positive effects including improved mood, overcoming sleeplessness. Another persistent myth is that masturbation will hinder sexual performance. Dr. Nicole Prause, a neuroscientist, who has thoroughly researched the subject and how it affects the brain, notes that "Every doctor and psychologist I spoke with informed me that 'there's no evidence' to link masturbation to sexual performance."

Masturbation is *not* a moral failure. It does *not* indicate that you are a "sex addict," a label that, as I mentioned earlier, is increasingly understood to be invalid and a misnomer. The late sex therapist, Jack Morin, said that whether one is struggling with the issue of masturbation and porn use, one's sexual identity, or other sexual issues perceived as pathological, going to war with these things is *not* the way to go. Trying to abstain from some form of sexual expression often leads to an *increase* in the behavior.

There is a Reddit forum called NoFap on which men challenge themselves and each other to abstain from masturbating to porn in an effort to "reboot" their sexual desire for a partner, others, or maybe just their self-esteem. The prevalent belief there is that the brain becomes hijacked by porn, and lessens desire for social and sexual contact, and that abstinence will reinvigorate one's sense of masculinity and sense of well-being.

There is scant evidence, other than anecdotal, that confirms this viewpoint. Also prevalent in this view is that self-pleasuring is not "real sex." One neuroscientist, Dr. Nicole Prause, who has thoroughly researched the subject and how it affects the brain has attempted to bust this myth. "Every doctor and psychologist I spoke with informed me that 'there's no evidence' to link masturbation to sexual performance, although ejaculating now may make it more difficult to ejaculate again immediately," she says.

In fact, she notes that studies show ejaculation increases fertility, and frequent ejaculation can lead to less risk of erectile dysfunction in later life.

Masturbation isn't the problem

The contrast between these two viewpoints brings me to what I've learned in my practice of relationship therapy—excessive watching of porn and masturbation is a *symptom, not the problem* in couples' sexual relations.

Think about it.

Masturbation for men and women is easy because it's all about you. In heterosexual couples, it is often the woman that has a problem with her male partner masturbating while watching porn. She often takes it personally as if he wants the porn and the women in it over her. But the truth is more likely that porn never says no. It never has a headache or requires sensitivity to a partner's level of comfort or their turn-ons. You don't need to set a date on the calendar to engage in it, it can start or stop anytime you want it to. If women are using sex toys to stimulate their clitoris, they never have to worry about a penis staying hard or getting in the right position. They may still complain that they are being replaced by their partner's porn, but then men could also complain that they have been replaced by a vibrator.

On the other hand, relationships are hard, especially around issues of intimacy, which require open and honest communication and negotiation. It is easier to talk with a stranger about sex than it is with our own partner. Why? Because the stakes are much higher. We fear that if we reveal our fantasies or what feels good to us, we may offend or create more distance between ourselves and our partner. Mostly I find that fear to be unfounded.

If, however, one is relying excessively on masturbation as a sexual release, especially if they are in a relationship, then it may be time to search for a better balance between self-pleasuring and relational sex. In my practice as a sex therapist, I find that these two things can coexist in a healthy way if someone is willing to do the work. It's true that in masturbation a man's penis can get accustomed to his hand, or women may become accustomed to her hand or sex toy, habituating the body to you and not your partner. But to get to the point where one's sexual attention can also be balanced with the relationship, one may have to overcome some barriers.

A good way to begin is to find the time and space to have these vulnerable and frank conversations. I facilitate such conversations in a therapeutic situation and encourage couples to make time for open conversations about sex at home. Ideally such conversations should have taken place in the beginning of the relationship, but too often they only come about when the relationship reaches a crisis point.

It takes maturity and ability to listen to one's partner non-judgmentally, to not take things personally, and to keep reactivity out of the discussion. The goal is to get a glimpse of the partner's inner sexual world through their eyes. Here are some examples of how healthy sexual conversations might get started:

- What satisfies you? What would you like me to do more of?
- During the act of making love, can we tell each other what we like, whether something needs to be harder or softer, where touching feels the best?
- Can we talk openly about concerns and fears about things such as penis size, stamina, or ejaculation, vaginal tightness or pain?
- Are we willing to be vulnerable and share the kinds of visual porn or erotic literature (what some women call "cliterature") that most turns either of us on? There is now even a website (www.sexionnaire.com) where each partner can separately enter the kinds of sexual things they like, and the site will report back to them *only* the ones they share in common.

EROTIC ORIENTATION

- Can we make time for conversations about our sexual fantasies and desires, and set aside time for sexual exploration? Many people regularly make appointments for having affairs, so why not do this with each other?
- Can you consider that even though your partner may be interested in viewing other people having sex, this is not cheating or a reason to think the partner is more interested in someone else? Rather, it is adding to or exploring their sexual interests and may signal a desire to explore the possibility of adding variety to their sex life. I remind couples that they have chosen the other as the partner, and that within this there are many ways that exploring sexuality can enhance that bond.

EROTIC ORIENTATION

6 MONOGAMY, POLYAMORY, AND CONSENSUAL NON-MONOGAMY ((NM)

Couples often fight over contracts they've never made.
— Mary Klein, sex therapist

When I sit down with couples, I ask them if they are monogamous, open, poly, monogamish or some other agreement they have made (Consensual non-monogamy is the newest term to describe open relationships to help understand that this is not about cheating. There is consent from both partners over the openness of their relationship). Even if they tell me they are monogamous I still ask them, "Have you negotiated your monogamy?" They often look at me like I'm crazy and wonder what that means. Most monogamous couples have neither talked about nor negotiated what monogamy means for them. They believe that if you have chosen monogamy you don't have to talk about it, and that each partner knows what this means, that there is a "normal" or the unspoken but universally understood standard of relationship exclusivity. It is known as *monoganormativity*.

This is an error. For some partners, looking at pornography is cheating. For others, masturbating feels like a betrayal. And for others, engaging in sexting or cybersex without ever meeting each other or even being in the same country is cheating. Monogamy demands discussion over its meaning just like any other relationship agreement.

For instance, I worked with a gay male couple who told me that they were monogamous. After several months, however, they informed me they had had a three-way. When I asked if they had changed from monogamy, they said, "No." I was confused. Maybe I hadn't gotten the correct information in our initial consultation? "I thought you told me you were monogamous," I said. "We are," they said. Now I was REALLY confused! "But you just told me you were monogamous!" "We are," they replied. "We only have three-ways together and are never sexual with others apart from each other."

Okay, now I was slowly getting it.

While "sleeping around" and "casually dating" are fairly common in today's world, open relationships and polyamory are still hard for most of society to understand—though millennials are catching on pretty quickly. Research is now classifying polyamory as its own orientation.

What is "normal"

One of the phrases we often hear in these chaotic times is "the new normal"—in other words, what was once considered an unquestioned standard has evolved into something we couldn't have imagined before. Especially when it comes to sexual matters, among the general public there are numerous layers of mistaken assumptions about what is "normal" and acceptable. We sex therapists, however, quickly come to understand that there are dozens, likely hundreds, or perhaps an endless amount of sexual behaviors that are "normal" in society but seldom openly discussed.

The common misconception about this is that people who have consensual non-monogamy or are polyamorous are "sex hungry" and just want to constantly be having a good time. The truth is that these types of relationships actually take hard work and a lot of honest communication. Whether it's a straight couple that are both flirting and/or openly sleeping with people on the side, or a lesbian "throuple" (a poly relationship with three people) where all three women have emotional and sexual relationships with each other, there has to be a lot of trust, open conversation, and safe sex occurring for these relationships to thrive, and they can and do.

We are taught that monogamy is the gold standard and anything that strays from it is problematic and wrong. However, if you are not monogamous nor want to be, you are judged and often seen as having something off about you. If monogamy is right for you in your relationship and it works, you still need to discuss what monogamy means to each of you.

As I've said, most monogamous couples I see have never talked about or negotiated what monogamy actually means for them—usually something as vague as "being loyal to one another." But when you begin to ask about specifics, they often have different ideas and have never talked about them.

When it comes to open relationships, in sex therapy there is no judgment despite society's idea that if a couple is open to bringing in others for sex, it's the beginning of the end of their relationship. In reality, many happy and successful relationships have open contracts around sex. Meanwhile, some monogamous couples struggle and disintegrate for not being willing to open up their relationships at all.

Open relationships are controversial, to be sure. Research shows that some 50 percent of gay male couples can manage open relationships successfully. Heterosexual couples, on the other hand, who have "assumed" monogamy rarely have talked openly about their sex lives before the infidelity, and often their lives are torn apart.

It is essential, then, to have clear, honest and open communication, and consensual agreement between partners, regardless of their sexual orientation.

Defining "monogamy"

Couples I have counseled have displayed a rather wide range of understanding about what monogamy means to them. Some examples:

Consensual Monogamy—Here, both partners agree openly and honestly about keeping their relationship monogamous and have a mutual definition of what that means. Both partners should discuss and agree on what monogamy means to them—usually sexual and emotional intimacy with each other, and no one else. If either or both want to open the relationship to others, it's with the understanding that they'll both discuss changing the contract through intentional dialogue and both agree on it. This is something that could take many conversations. One hesitant partner should never agree, and the other partner should never push too hard.

Consensual non-monogamy (CNM)—Books on affairs have been exploding in the self-help market in the past 10 years. This seems to acknowledge the lack of conversation and openness amongst couples, which leads to a rupture in the relationship and exits from intimacy. However, attitudes about monogamy are slowly showing signs of changing. For instance, at a recent talk I gave on same-sex marriage, a group of CEOs challenged me on the concept. One man in particular asked, "If we open the doors to gay marriage, then what's next—polygamy?" Another man in the group looked at him and asked, "How could you be against polygamy? You've divorced three wives and are looking for a fourth!"

For an open sexual and/or emotional relationship with others, mutual consent of both partners is essential. Here, each agrees to open the relationship in ways satisfactory to both. Some partners prefer not to know about their partner's sexual behavior outside the relationship. They have a "don't ask, don't tell" policy; others want to know, and many insist on knowing. Rules are important here. I have heard male couples say, "We only do it on vacation," or "only with people we don't know." Working this out is imperative.

While "hooking up" and "casually dating" are fairly normal in today's dating world, open relationships and polyamory remain controversial to be sure and are still hard for most of society to accept—though millennials are catching on pretty quickly. While 50 percent of gay male couples manage open relationships successfully, heterosexual couples that have "assumed" monogamy can find their lives torn apart because of affairs and cheating. Only rarely do these couples talk openly about their sex lives before the infidelity. This is far worse than a couple talking openly and honestly with each other about a sensitive topic like sexuality from the beginning.

Here are some essential elements of making contracts in relationships:

Staying true to contract. Never assume there's a contract on sexual exclusivity. Any couple should understand that by itself, being married and/or in a relationship isn't enough to ensure monogamy. Each may have different ideas about what "marriage" and "relationship" means. It's vital for the couple to mutually agree on a contract stating their agreement about monogamy, or non-monogamy.

Breaking the relationship agreement. This occurs if one or both partners stray from the agreed-upon contract. The relationship would not be in trouble over the affair as much as about the contract, consciously and intentionally prepared by both partners.

Safer sex. There is no such thing as safe sex unless it is with yourself! We now say "safer sex" to help people remember that whenever you engage in sexual activity with another person you are at risk for contracting an STI. When sexually playing outside their relationships, couples need to be are cautious about STIs. The idea is to assume that everybody else is may have a sexually transmitted infection or disease and act accordingly. It's neither appropriate nor realistic to hope the person you're with is telling you the truth—or how recently he's been tested. Play safely, no matter what.

Fidelity without sexual exclusivity. In their book, *The Male Couple*, David P. McWhirter, M.D., and Andre M. Mattison, MSW, Ph.D., write that among male couples, "Sexual exclusivity ... is infrequent, yet their expectations of fidelity are high. Fidelity is not defined in terms of sexual behavior but rather by their emotional commitment to each other."

Renegotiating a contract. Another thought that couples have found helpful is to not make any contracts in stone! Theirs can be a living relationship that is open and closed at various points in time, with no hard rules about it. It's more important to know when and how to discuss desired changes in the contract.

Maintaining intentional dialogue. Effective dialogue is the best thing couples can do to ensure safety and trust. The best form of communication I have found is called the *intentional dialogue*, developed by Dr. Harville Hendrix and explained in his book, *Getting the Love You Want*. One partner is the receiver, and the other is the sender. One partner at a time speaks, and the other listens actively by reflecting back what was heard. This guarantees there won't be any judgments, interruptions, interpretations, or reactivity and defensiveness during a partner's sharing. The sender should speak only in "I" statements and talk about personal feelings and judgments, never presuming to know what the other person thinks. This kind of respect and communication is essential for any open relationship.

Jealousy from consensual non-monogamy. Whether couples are in closed or open relationships, jealousy is bound to rear its head. I've heard couples, gay and straight, voice their anxiety that their partner liked the other person more, enjoyed some sexual behavior from the other person more, and so on. Again, resolving this requires dialogue and safety between the partners. Knowing in advance the kinds of issues that an open relationship may present can help prevent some of these conflicts in the first place.

You might think that having multiple romantic partners would elicit more jealousy than being in a monogamous relationship. But according to a 2017 study published in *Perspectives on Psychological Science*, that's not necessarily the case.

The study, which surveyed 1,507 people in monogamous relationships and 617 people in consensual non-monogamous relationships, found that people in consensual non-monogamous relationships, including those who engaged in polyamory and swinging, scored lower on jealousy and higher on trust than those in monogamous relationships.

"People in monogamous relationships were really off the charts high on jealousy. They were more likely to check their partners' phones, go through their emails, their handbags," one of the authors of the study says. "But people in consensual non-monogamous relationships were really low on this." Another of the authors, who also works as a couples therapist, says that she's observed monogamous couples avoid addressing jealousy altogether, whereas consensual non-monogamous couples might be more vocal with their feelings. "In consensual non-monogamous relationships, jealousy is expected," she says. "But they see what feelings arise and actively work to navigate them in a proactive way."

To sum up, "normal" remains in the eye of the beholder—the individual and the couple. Especially for therapists it's not appropriate to judge couples for behavior that society does not believe to be "proper" for any relationship. The therapist can

EROTIC ORIENTATION

question the couple about open relationships and share their thoughts and concerns. However, if the arrangement is working for them, then the therapist needs to stand back and let them make the final decisions.

7 EMOTIONAL LANDSCAPE AND ATTACHMENT

Tell me how you were loved as a child and I will tell you how you make love as an adult.

—Esther Perel, sex therapist and author

As I discussed earlier, early attachment and bonding experiences shape your later ability to attach and bond with others. We sex therapists understand that these same attachments and experiences help develop and shape sexual fantasies in adulthood.

Remember that these are not to be confused with sexual orientation—how you identify yourself as straight, gay, lesbian, bisexual, or otherwise. *Sexual and romantic orientations* are who you are inherently at your core. *Erotic orientation,* on the other hand, is learned and shaped more by how you were raised and the types of relationships you witnessed in childhood.

Many sexual preferences are imprinted, beginning in childhood when your sexual map is determined. We observe and absorb how others love, neglect, or abuse us—and that becomes our "love map," or template for what we seek out for pleasure as adults.

In *Arousal: The Secret Logic of Sexual Fantasies*, Dr. Michael Bader writes, "The unconscious management of psychological safety does not begin with the onset of mature sexual desires. It begins in childhood, almost from the moment of birth. As research now tells us, the newborn baby is wired to form an attachment to its mother. The baby can recognize the mother's particular voice and face and prefers them to all other voices and faces. Evolution has guaranteed that the baby has the ability and desire to connect to the human being most able to help it survive. Furthermore, our brains and psychological natures are primed to make us love those people who are responsible for our well-being.

"We become attached, and we fall in love. Without such attachment, psychological research has shown that babies become frantic, disorganized, and depressed. A secure attachment is crucial to healthy psychological development."

Attachment to a parent figure is the first crucial stage of development. How you learn to attach and bond sets the stage for your later relationships. It also sets the stage for your later sexual content and fantasies. To understand your erotic orientation, you must learn who your attachment figures were and how they were with you during this developmental time when you were learning to attach.

- Were your attachment figures smothering or distant and disengaged?
- Did you feel like you were a burden on your parents?
- Did they grant your wishes, or did you have to grant their wishes?
- Did they allow you your independence growing up or was that discouraged?

If your parents were unhappy, depressed, and unavailable and you responded by trying not to upset them or demand too much, then you may be working out these conflicts within your erotic landscape. In *Arousal*, Bader writes about people in sexual fantasies being happy; in the sexual sphere, everyone is pleased—no depressed mother, a "giving" parent, a sense of belonging unlike that which you might have had in your family.

A good example of this is my client Tomas, a Hispanic

man who came into my office troubled over a sexual fantasy he had of a watching women amputees. He didn't even need to watch porn to get aroused, he just watched YouTube videos of women walking around with missing limbs. He felt ashamed of this and worried he was sexually objectifying these women who were suffering and thought something was wrong with him. I explained to him that most of our sexual fantasies come from our childhood and then did a history of how he was raised.

    His father died when he was 8 and he was a raised by a single, divorced mother as an only child. His mother was deeply depressed throughout his childhood. Because of her depression she could not work. No amount of therapy or medication was helpful to her. She even went through electroconvulsive therapy (ECT), which did not help her depression. She was in and out of hospitals, and he felt very bad for her. He catered to her, went shopping for the family, cleaned the house and took care of the laundry. Tomas even took on two jobs outside of school to help keep their apartment. His mother was on social security disability so there was some income. Watching his mother depressed brought him much pain and anguish.

    Next door to where he lived was a woman who had an amputated leg. She worked full time and lived alone. He would often offer to help her carry in her groceries or shovel her sidewalk, but she always declined and did it all on her own. He watched in her in awe and recalls wishing his mother was as physically able as this neighbor was.

    Now things became clear. Tomas was in emotional pain and depression of his own with his mother. The woman next door was someone he wished his mother was. When his erotic orientation surfaced, he unconsciously he eroticized the neighbor woman to anesthetize the emotional pain of having a depressed, immobilized mother. The women amputees in his fantasies were really the woman next door whom he found to be potent and strong, unlike his mother who has all her limbs.

EROTIC ORIENTATION

Once Tomas understood this, he could have erotic empathy for himself. The shame of his interest in amputated women was now gone and he actually decided that he wanted to consciously date women who were amputees.

EROTIC ORIENTATION

8 SEXUAL FANTASIES AND INTEGRITY/EROTIC INTELLIGENCE

Sexual fantasies allow us to set integrity and political correctness aside. Things we would never do or say in reality we get to do in our fantasies. Paying careful attention to your sexual desires, erotic needs, and sexual fantasies can help you learn a great deal about what you're looking for in a partner and want to receive in a relationship.

The details of your sexual fantasies don't matter as much as their themes—an important distinction lest you get lost looking at the details and not be able to see the forest for the trees. Again, following the themes is like interpreting a dream. The details seem silly, but the symbolism is full of information about you. Whether you have healthy or unhealthy sexual desires, fantasies, or behaviors, it is for your benefit to understand what they represent for you.

As Guy Kettelhack writes in *Dancing Around the Volcano*, "Sexual symptoms and fixations are the psyche's energetic and ingenious attempts to cure itself—to give itself what it craves." That is, sexual fantasies and erotic desires are not pathological, but a form of self-help—erotic blueprints that can help you know yourself more deeply and discover the right partner.

I worked with a woman client who loved being spanked and couldn't find a partner who was willing to indulge this desire. Eventually she sought out a group of people who also shared this fantasy and was able to enact it with no judgment. As a child she may have been physically punished as a form of discipline causing her to resent her parents control over her.

Her asking a partner to spank her puts her in control, unlike what happened to her as a child. In sexual fantasy and play—like she is doing with the spanking groups—the desire can be satisfied on a temporary basis. That is the cleverness of erotic moments. I suspect she was fantasizing a parental figure in this. There's nothing intrinsically wrong with this unless she forgets this is play and actually sees her spanker as a parental figure.

If you ask a hundred different people about their sexual fantasies and preferences, you will get a hundred different answers—many *quite* different—and each response will tell you about that person and their personal history. Certain things, even trivial ones, may be important in arousing one person, whereas the same fantasy might turn off someone else.

That is because everyone's history, childhood, and socialized imprints are different. Each of us has his own erotic thumbprint/erotic orientation, which become erotic blueprints for arousal, cleverly reenacting the original disturbing event, this time with a happy ending. It may be difficult for clients to reveal their sexual fantasies and interests in therapy, but once they do, we find plenty of information about them. Compulsive sexual behaviors by those who let themselves be ruled by sexual fantasy instead of being in control of it, can interfere with finding a partner and entering a relationship. But if in therapy I can uncover the non-sexual aspects of disguised material or "story," then I can help them.

The case of Aaron

Aaron was a heterosexual male who was about to be married when he came into some legal trouble. He was arrested for approaching adult women in mall parking lots, flashing them with his erect penis, making gestures with his tongue, then getting in his car and speeding away. He was an exhibitionist, someone who primarily gets aroused by exhibiting his genitals to others. One upset woman took down his license plate and called the police. Arrested, he admitted to this sexual behavior. He was puzzled as well as ashamed of it and couldn't figure out why he was doing this. In my office he admitted having done it for some time, and increasingly more often since his engagement and upcoming wedding. Now he faced the shame of telling his fiancée what he had done and the risk of losing her.

In looking into his past, we discovered that his mother had been very dominant and controlling while his father was passive and distant. If Aaron made any attempts to voice his thoughts, the women in the family would tell him to be quiet. He felt stifled and emasculated.

Again, as Esther Perel stated, "Tell me how you were loved as a child and I will tell you how you make love as an adult." The way he had been loved (or lack thereof) as a child had manifested into how he was expressing sexually as an adult. His sexual fantasies and desires had resolved these feelings by showing these anonymous women what a "man" he was. His tongue gestures let her know he could use his mouth and could pleasure her with it, whereas his family hadn't wanted him to open his mouth to talk and basically gagged him. The women he flashed were stand-ins for the women in his family.

His work then, determined by the erotic impulses that we uncovered, was to assert himself more with the women in his life. It turned out (not surprisingly) that his fiancée was opinionated and had a dominant side. At work, with female superiors and co-workers, he did the same thing, returning to the scene of the crime by recreating his family dynamics. His sexuality was telling him, "You need to express yourself and your masculinity to women," and channeled it through his sexual behavior by his exhibitionism.

Aaron did, in fact, assert himself more to his wife, and their relationship improved. His wife had difficulty with this at first but adjusted. His changed behavior did little to repair relationships with some family members, but he built a stronger relationship with his father. Ultimately, although the thought of showing his penis to unsuspecting women still aroused him, he no longer did so. His erotic fantasies no longer ruled him; he had mastered them.

An important point: *All* sexual fantasies are healthy

Everyone has voyeuristic/exhibitionist tendencies at some level. But fantasies like Aaron's should never be acted on because they might put the one who has them (or someone else) at risk. This isn't an issue for most people because it is not primary or a part of their core erotic orientation.

Some people discover, for example, that sex with sex workers is a form of "paying for love," and that is erotic for them. As children, they either weren't loved or loved enough by their caregivers. To be loved as children they may have become honor students, doing extra chores around the house, becoming the most obedient child all to just be loved and noticed by a caretaker or parent who still doesn't recognize them or show them the love they deserve. These are acts of "paying" for love in behavioral ways. To do so financially can become a way of reconciling it in the erotic realm and might also ameliorate some of the guilt of hiring a hooker.

Other people may want to dominate and be in charge since they often feel helpless and powerless in life. Some like to be humiliated by golden showers, being spit on, and verbally abused, possibly because they struggle with maintaining a sense of pride in themselves. Sometimes men who are CEOs or in powerful positions of great responsibility will seek out someone who will dominate and humiliate them, or they fantasize about it. This seems to provide a sort of psychic balance, allowing them to remove the burden of always being in charge.

None of this means that you have to stop your fantasies or change the desires or behaviors these play out. It does mean that if you want to feel more powerful and take more pride in your life, you can find ways to be loved without paying for it.

Rape and incest fantasies

Much of porn centers on rape fantasies: the hot military/police/boss/coach/teacher or another individual in authority who forces themselves onto another person, with both ultimately enjoying it. For those who want to be dominated, this allows them to feel accepted by a dominant masculine man and provides them with a way to feel good about what's happening to them, and studies show that a high percentage of straight women have rape fantasies. This doesn't mean they *want* to be raped. For them, I suspect, it's a way of sexualizing the male dominance and patriarchy in their lives. In the fantasy it is "play rape" and everyone is enjoying themselves unlike real rape which is never about sex and the victim is never enjoying themselves.

This can also be true about men who want to be dominated by women for the same reasons in that they want to feel a loss of control, a sense of vulnerability, and can give up control to a woman.

Those who want to dominate have similar issues from the other side. Dominating someone else might give them a sense of control and power they don't always have access to in their everyday lives.

We will talk more about this in the next section where I unpack BDSM (Bondage, Discipline, Sadomasochism, and Submission).

Again, there's nothing wrong with these fantasies and nothing wrong with play-acting them out. I want to help clients explore in a positive way *why* they've developed that *particular* fantasy.

What about incest stories, which are found often in straight, gay, and bisexual porn? If a parent was depressed, disengaged, and unavailable during a child's formative years, then an incest fantasy of a parent being sexual with the adult child can help banish the sadness and longings remaining from childhood. The sexualized connection of the fantasy lets both the fantasy parent figure and/or sibling, and fantasy adult child experience a tight-knit bond, even though it is acted upon only in fantasy.

In other words, the lack of love and feeling of neglect in childhood becomes resolved in the erotic fantasy. I see this a lot amongst gay men who are into daddy/son fantasies and role playing. It is a way to play with unresolved issues for the person who has unhealed wounds from childhood. Also, as Bader points out, you can't be sexually aroused and unhappy at the same time. So again, in this parent-adult child fantasy, everyone is happily turned on. Sadness and longing are banished.

This is a far better explanation for sexual fantasies and arousal than attributing them to pathology and sickness. The human psyche is always looking to repair itself and return to wholeness, so it's not surprising that it would use erotica and the sexual realm as corrective tools.

Pain vs pleasure

Our capacity to eroticize nearly anything can be shocking to someone unfamiliar with this idea that eroticism springs from the psyche's attempt to heal childhood wounds. It is particularly difficult to understand for those have felt no attraction to the eroticism of bondage, domination, and sadomasochism (BDSM). Many therapists have a negative response to someone who has eroticized feelings around power and control. But many people do find BDSM erotic—in seemingly endless variations—and they have truly found their erotic identity in such practices and fantasies. They've learned to transcend their past rather than having it inflicted upon them. Just as an artist may use past trauma to express herself in her work, she may use past trauma to express herself in the bedroom. Nobody tries to get an artist to stop expressing past traumas.

Many therapists will keep a client in therapy for years "helping" to get rid of unwanted sexual desires and fantasies—especially if that client is non-normative and non-heterosexual. Let's face it, for the unscrupulous therapist, sexual taboos can be an untapped goldmine. We have seen this with so-called conversion therapists, burying facts and lying to clients (and desperately homophobic parents of clients) about changing sexual orientation from gay to straight. But while there is a strong consensus in the psychological community against conversion therapy, there is no such strong consensus against "curing" BDSM sexuality. This exists despite the fact that no creditable scientific study has shown any trend of psychological pathologies in people drawn to BDSM.

In 2013, BDSM activities were removed as "disorders" from the Diagnostic and Statistical Manual (DSM-5, 2013) used for diagnosing mental disorders. What remains are codes for those struggling with unwanted sexual fantasies and desires. If we as psychotherapists ask ourselves, "Why is this sexual behavior unwanted?" the answer is likely because our culture and world demonizes sexual desires, often attaching them unconsciously to violent and offending behaviors.

Was someone shamed a lot as a child by parents or others? If so, you often will find such people erotically engaging in acts of humiliation, being spoken to in shaming ways, and so on. In one sense this is reenactment of childhood trauma, but instead of being harmful or traumatizing, feeling that shame again in a sexual context has transformed it into something pleasurable and healing.

Was someone forced to be responsible in his family for things at too early an age, and he continues this in life as a CEO or someone with power over others? He may find it erotic to be sexually powerless, dominated and controlled by a woman making him crawl on all fours and do her bidding.

Was someone subjected to repeated physical pain by a parent or a guardian? Then they very well may seek out someone who, in a controlled situation, will inflict bodily pain while they are immobilized with ropes or handcuffs enduring such practices as whipping, caning, spanking, nipple clips, being slapped, and so on. This is sadomasochism, a widely practiced form of erotic play. There are even conventions held around the nation that take over an entire hotel and set up rooms like dungeons or caves where you can explore what turns you on.

Again, following the principles of sexual health, these must be consensual experiences, and limits (or no limits) agreed upon before the play begins. The painful childhood experience thus has become eroticized and therefore pleasurable. As has often been said, there is a fine line between pain and pleasure. For some, pain is exciting. They experience more powerful orgasms when accompanied by pain. Those who participate in such meetings have found their erotic identity in such places. Of course, because we have the ability to imagine, some people will never put themselves in a situation like this but become highly aroused thinking about it during sex.

Even blackmail can be eroticized. I had a client whose wife discovered that her husband was engaging in sex talk and display online. Even worse in her mind was that the person he was interacting with would frequently threaten the husband by telling him she would reveal his secret life to his wife, his children, and all his friends if he didn't pay her money. What we found out in couples therapy was that it was all just play stemming from his mother's habit of confiding in him, telling him if he ever told his father these secrets that the father would leave them, and they would be homeless, a form of blackmail. His psyche was able to turn this trauma into erotic experience. He was quite turned on by such talk, and no money was ever really exchanged.

Money can play many roles in eroticism. If in childhood someone experienced much stress around money—for instance not having enough of it and always in fear of being poor—then paying for sex can be a turn on. Or, as in the example above, being threatened with losing one's money to a blackmailer becomes exciting. Or when the only way someone's parents expressed love was with money. There is even a character with an online business who specializes in working with people who have these blackmail fantasies...and makes a living at it!

Then there is the erotic imagining of one's partner having sex with someone else. This is sometimes referred to as "hotwifing," which I address further in the next chapter. One of my clients told me that when he first started dating the woman who became his wife, he got turned on by her stories of sex with other men she had previously dated. When he came into my office they had been married and in love for 20 years, but in recent years their sex life had suffered because he found it more and more difficult to get turned on. Then his wife came home and went on and on about a co-worker flirting with her. Suddenly the husband was turned on thinking about his wife having sex with this co-worker, and he was ashamed and confused about it. When we delved into his childhood, we were able to connect this fantasy to the fact that his mother had multiple boyfriends after divorcing his father. She always told him he was her "number one guy," but then he would see her with multiple men with whom she dated and had sex with. We were able to see that he was jealous of these men his mother dated. Now the men his wife had dated and slept with, and this co-worker, were stand-ins for the men his mother was with. He had eroticized the jealousy. When he finally came to realize that this was part of him, his erotic orientation, he wept, relieved to know himself in a way he had never before acknowledged.

Again, eroticizing early traumas is a common way of healing from those experiences. Not all people who are into BDSM have a major trauma or abuse history. However, many do. Many therapists wrongly refer to this as trauma reenactment and focus on what happened in childhood that made someone interested in kinky play. But the term reenactment should only apply in cases where the adult returns to the scene of the crime unconsciously seeking to correct it—or to remain emotionally trapped and stunted. In cases of BDSM play, however, the return is consciously manipulated or played with to enhance a sexual experience. Period. There need be no angst or shaming involved. And no need for years of therapy to correct.

It is also important to remember that kink is not a diagnosis. Also, not all kinks and fetishes come from childhood traumas or negative experiences.

Now let's talk about erotic differences and how they can affect intimacy.

EROTIC ORIENTATION

9 SEXUAL INTIMACY AND EROTIC DIFFERENCES

Another of the most common reasons couples come into my office is due to erotic differences. While therapists across the board are taught how to help couples work through their differences by having empathy for one another about how to raise kids, spend money, where to live, etc., erotic differentiation is rarely something that gets attention. The goal is to help couples have *erotic empathy* toward one another, understanding that each has their own erotic orientation that neither threatens each other nor takes away from the relationship.

Erotic empathy
Sex therapist, Amanda Luterman, MA, M.ED, talks about erotic empathy. She writes, *"Erotic empathy* is the ability to allow your partner to find you attractive even when you don't feel you are. It is the active practice of accepting that your partner can experience you in a light that you yourself do not see nor understand. Erotic empathy, specifically, is the skill of empathic perspective-taking while in a state of erotic connection. Empathy, outside of eroticism, is the ability to see something through the perspective of someone else; it is a non-judgmental interest in their lived experience." (https://medium.com/@amandaluterman/i-am-carrot-cake-a-lesson-in-erotic-empathy-a33cebe33c14)

In the case of relationships. What I am encouraging is for couples to have erotic empathy toward their partners and also toward themselves.

Heterosexual couples usually do not explicitly talk about their erotic interests from the beginning of a relationship the way gay male couples do. Gay males will actually put in their profile exactly what they are looking for sexually and erotically first before the romantic interests. This is often to avoid the painful discovery that while they may be in love and together for many years they are erotically at odds and different. This cannot assure it won't happen at all, as erotic interests change and evolve over time, but it greatly reduces the pain of a surprise revelation that the couple has these differences.

When couples do not discuss their erotic interests from the beginning of their relationship, they often hope it will work out later. It often doesn't. By the time they reveal these interests to their spouse they may have no interest and now have to negotiate what to do, which can be difficult to talk about and resolve.

Typically, when one partner wants something sexually and the other says no, therapists align with the partner with whom they are more comfortable, most often the one who's saying "no." But this is not something that can be fixed with a quick aligning with one partner over the other. All partners involved need to talk through their differences and work through them together until everyone is satisfied.

Emotional connection

Sexual contact with another person can get confused with a genuine emotional connection. Many people use sex to fill a void in their lives and to feel wanted, but sexual contact alone is *not* love. While it can help couples stay close to each other and let individuals release their libido, the rest of their relational work needs to happen outside the sexual realm. In other words, even though sexual contact might fulfill your psyche somehow, it's no replacement for the work necessary to attach to a partner and have real love—which isn't easy. Sex offers instant pleasure, but true sexual and romantic intimacy takes work. If you're not doing that work, the relational intimacy is often shallow and superficial.

EROTIC ORIENTATION

I often meet clients who were raised in families in which there was no outward expression of affection. They'll explain away this lack of expression as the "WASP way" or "a German thing" or "the way of the English folk." They'll tell me they never doubted they were—and are—loved by their parents but were never shown its outward expressions. I begin to help them understand that while they logically understand that they're loved, a part of the brain doesn't understand. Lack of demonstrative affection can often make children feel emotionally neglected. These children are starving for direct affection and act out in ways to get it somewhere else.

Sex and emotional attachment

One couple with whom I worked often participated in "hotwifing" in which the wife goes out and flirts with other men. It turned the husband on to watch his wife turn other men on and have sex with them. The husband might be watching, or she could be texting him about what's happening as he masturbates at home. She may or may not bring the new guy back with her. If she does, the husband may continue masturbating while watching the two engage in foreplay and/or sex, join them for group sex, or have the wife come back to him to have "the hottest sex ever." Same-sex couples also participate in hotwifing (there is no comparable name at this time) depending on which partner will be aroused by watching and which is interested in being intimate with a third party.

In the case of this couple, the wife was not sure at first if she wanted to do it, saying that her husband was enough for her. The husband said, "I know in my heart that I am enough for you, but in my mind it's erotic to me for us to play that I'm *not* enough for you." They had several sexually healthy conversations and agreements, and eventually she did go out to flirt with other men, text her husband pictures, etc., to get him excited before she came back to have sex with both men or just her husband. She found that the whole experience turned her on. She felt safe with the first guy, a stranger, but then the husband can potentially become jealous that she might develop an emotional attachment to the stranger. Hotwifing requires the male and female partners to have ongoing sexual health dialogues with each other and even take "time outs" from the sex act to assess where they each are in dealing with the fantasy and the reality. With the couple I was working with, the wife was able to separate sex with the new man from the love she has for her husband, but her husband was not convinced that she could do it successfully, despite her proclamations to the contrary.

Women often discover they enjoy hotwifing but have cognitive dissonance around this. She sees herself as the monogamous "good girl" she was raised to be but now also someone who likes to be objectified and have anonymous sex. She is often slut-shamed for this while men tend not to be, a double standard, unfortunately, rooted in our sexist society. While boys are encouraged to go out, "play the field" and have a list of sexual encounters that is longer than the number of relationships they've been in, women are socialized to not separate sex from love, though they have just as much capacity to do so. If there is no emotional attachment, women are degraded for being overly sexual. In our culture monogamy, especially for women, is the correct and "normal" way to have relationships, as I previously discussed. We shame anyone who does not commit to a relationship, such as couples who have various types of open relationships, or who are polyamorous.

Looking deeper into the husband's childhood, we found that as one out of ten siblings, he did not get much attention, and this led to him eroticizing not being enough for his partner. The work we did to heal his childhood wounds of not being chosen and not feeling like he *was* enough helped him to understand why he desired hotwifing. This couple's issue was that even when we had uncovered the *why,* the desire remained but could not be acted upon while the husband continued to feel jealous. This, then, was not a sex issue, but a trust issue.

The therapy was now about working on trust and not pathologizing the hotwifing fantasy they both enjoyed. I helped them both see that from his childhood trusting that people would be there for him and not abandon him was being played out between them. This happens to all couples whether sexually or non-sexually and is an opportunity to heal unresolved childhood wounds. This couple was able to do this by talking things through and arriving at earned trust based on their secure attachment to each other.

If you keep the communication strong and listen to each other, couples can work through issues of dividing sex from intimacy to the benefit of all parties.

Gary and Susan's erotic differences

Gary, a software engineer, and Susan, a college professor, had contacted me because they weren't happy with their sex life. In their mid-40s, they'd been married for 17 years and had a teenage son. In our first session, they sat on my couch holding hands, Gary dressed casually in slacks and a sport shirt and Susan more formally in a pant suit. Although they both looked rather apprehensive, from their proximity and willingness to exchange direct glances with each other, I felt that they were a loving couple.

When I asked them to say more about what brought them in, Gary spoke first. "Well, in the beginning of our relationship, we used to make love for hours," he said. "I'm actually a pretty romantic guy, and I liked doing all that tender stuff, but a few years ago, I began wanting to do more of the things I've always fantasized about."

Susan turned to me and said with a look of disgust, "He wants me to dress in high heels and black fishnet stockings and talk dirty in bed. I've done it for him many times, but the whole thing feels disrespectful to me. And then I found out that he's looking at women dressed like this in online porn. That's where I think he got the whole idea."

"That's not where it came from," Gary said. "I was just too embarrassed to tell you about it before. Actually, I did try to tell you before we were married, but you looked so insulted by the idea of it that I just let it go."

"Gary, how long have you been fantasizing about women in fishnet stockings?" I asked.

"My whole life. I used to take my mother's fishnet stockings and masturbate while holding them. Honestly, it's always turned me on."

"Well, it doesn't seem right that you need props to have sex with me," Susan interjected.

Gary turned to look directly at her. "Susan, I love you, and I love those clothes, and the bonus is when I see *you* wearing them. If you don't want to wear these things, I can live with that, but then I'm still going to get my needs met by looking at women online wearing the stockings. I'd rather be looking at you, though."

"I don't like that you'd look at that stuff online," she replied angrily, pulling her hand away from his. "My body should be enough for you the way it is."

"It *is*," Gary insisted, "but I'd like to have these extra things, too."

Here their power struggle over these erotic differences became clear. She doesn't want to have sex this way, and when she concedes, she feels her husband is more into the stockings and heels than her. Because Gary can tell she's turned off, he's turned off as well, putting a further damper on their sex life.

As therapists, we work hard at helping couples learn to accept each other's differences, but we rarely intervene in the same way for couples when it comes to sex. As I took their history, I could see that they were well differentiated as a couple in terms of everyday living, raising their son, and managing their finances.

However, they weren't well differentiated sexually. The first thing I needed to do to change this was to help them avoid getting stuck in a one-up and one-down position. In putting down Gary's erotic preferences, Susan was taking the morally dominant position, dismissing his way of experiencing attachment, even wanting to control his private watching of porn. To help them find a way out of their stalemate, I needed to help Susan understand something about fetishes like this.

"I can tell that this feels like a personal assault to you," I told her, "but you should know that men typically have more fetishes like this than women. Many of my male clients have sexual fantasies that don't involve their wives, only women to whom they feel no attachment, but what I'm hearing is that Gary wants to do this with *you*, not other women. That suggests to me that this is a way he wants to bond with you by exploring some of his fantasies with you." Gary nodded while I was speaking. "Can you hear that Gary is saying that it's not just about the clothes, that it's about you, too?"

"Maybe," she conceded, but then the look of disgust returned to her face. "But he also wants me to go on and on about how big his penis is, and how he wants me to swallow his ejaculate. That's vulgar to me. It's gutter talk. And the words he uses when we have sex to talk about my own body parts are utterly disrespectful. I wasn't brought up this way, and it completely turns me off."

"That makes sense to me that you feel this way," I said. Turning to Gary, I said, "Every day, women are fending off male advances—in the office, in the grocery store, while they're walking down the street. Much of the time, they feel objectified by predatory men, so naturally Susan is sensitive to this kind of disrespect, and she needs to hear romantic talk as well. Does it make sense to you that at times she needs you to stretch more toward her needs?"

"I know that's true," he responded rather sheepishly. "I've seen how other men look at her. I understand, and I don't want to make her feel that way. I really do try to let her know how I much I love and respect her, but I guess I can do a better job of that."

"To Susan I said, "You may be conflating that lewd guy in the grocery store, or wherever it is, with your husband. It's important to keep in mind that it's *you* Gary wants, not some anonymous woman on the street. For him, it's not about dominance or disrespect, but about how he expresses his attachment, as odd as that may seem to you right now. However, it's important for Gary to respect your boundaries. If you say something doesn't feel good, he needs to respect that and stop."

In the next session, Susan started. "I thought about what you said, so when Gary came home from work on Thursday, I greeted him at the door in those black stockings. He seemed really happy. But as soon as we went upstairs to the bedroom, he started in with his dirty talk. It ruined the mood completely. Instead of saying how much he loved that I did that for him, he told me all the things he wanted to do to me. I took those damn stockings off, put on my jeans, and I decided to walk the dog."

Gary shook his head. "I did appreciate it. All I said was that I wanted to fuck her hard and that I wanted her to suck me until I came. I thought after the last session it would be okay, but she freaked out. So, when she went to walk the dog, I watched some porn because I was all worked up and didn't know what else to do."

I took a deep breath and turned to Susan. "That's how many men talk sexually," I said, "how they express their attachment to their partners during sex. In the same way, women like to say things like 'take all of me' or 'ravish me' or 'tell me I'm the most beautiful woman you've ever seen.' One conveys words of love, and one is dirty talk—they're just different languages. He's speaking in objectified ways that allow him to be more turned on. You know, Susan, research indicates this is a way that men can separate their partner from, say, the mother of their children, and even from their own mother. When people are intimate, many times another persona comes out to play, one that's hidden from the rest of the world. With Gary, this other persona seems to say that he wants to trust you with this vulnerable, private part of himself, and hopes that you can get turned on, too. It's kind of a paradox: by objectifying you and talking dirty to you in bed as if you were a different person than you are in day-to-day life, he ends up feeling closer to you. He's revealing a glimpse of what I call his core sexual script and sharing it with you. Maybe it shouldn't be the only way he talks in bed, but can you perhaps consider it's one of the ways?"

Susan thought for a moment and seemed to soften. Then she said, "Well, I'm not okay with him looking at porn or masturbating when he has access to me. I think that when guys do that, they start wanting other women and going out to find them. He shouldn't have to do that."

I pointed to a book on my bookshelf, David Ley's well-researched and humorous book called *Ethical Porn for Dicks: A Man's Guide to Responsible Viewing Pleasure*. "This psychologist's research clearly shows that men enjoy both porn and sex with their partners, and don't replace one with the other. Think about books like *Twilight* and *Fifty Shades of Grey*," I said. "People call these 'cliterature' because they're a turn-on for women. They express a desire to imagine a partner who's more exciting than the person with whom they're sharing their bed. But having such fantasies doesn't have to mean that a woman will betray her husband with someone else, or that their relationship is somehow doomed. *It's just fantasy.*"

"Well, I guess I hadn't thought of that," she said, turning to Gary with the hint of a smile on her face. "Is that true?" she asked him.

"Yes!" Gary said. "Seeing the stuff online is just something that makes me horny. And it's a role I want to play with you. It excites me! *You* excite me!"

"But when you say the things you do, it's hard for me not to feel disrespected," she replied.

I interjected, "What if you were to turn this around, Susan? What if you were to take a dominant position and say something like 'I want your cock. It's mine. It belongs to me,' or 'Take all of me' or 'Fuck me now'? Many women who read romance novels find it sexy to imagine being ravished and possessed by an alpha man."

I asked Gary, "How would that feel to you? Could you handle that?"

"Oh, my God, yes!" he said. "That would turn me on for sure, and it would make me feel like you see and accept this part of me without all the judgment."

I said to Susan, "Do you think you might talk with some of your girlfriends and find out if any of them enjoy some of this kind of talk and behavior? I think you might be surprised by their answer."

"I guess I can do that," she said, smiling. "Maybe it's more normal than I thought."

"Again," I suggested, "think of your sexual encounters as play, like you're acting out different scenarios. You might find it exciting, and even grow closer as a result."

Over the months that followed, Gary reported that by experimenting with these roles, he was surprised that the passion and romantic feelings they had in the beginning of their relationship had reawakened, and they could again make tender love for hours. Susan reported awakening dormant sexual fantasies and thoughts she'd had as an adolescent, like slowly stripping off her clothes (all except the stockings and high heels) and masturbating for Gary. She bought more sexy bedroom outfits and some toys and gave herself permission to experiment with her sexual connection to Gary in ways she'd never dreamed of. They were grateful for their newfound pleasure and felt more bonded than ever.

So, ironically, Gary's erotic fantasies at first alienated Susan, driving the couple farther apart. But given the chance to explore these openly in a safe setting, they rediscovered the passion in their marriage.

(Portions of this chapter were previously published in Psychotherapy Networkers *magazine.)*

10 PROBLEMATIC SEXUAL BEHAVIOR

Throughout this book I have spoken to the idea of "healthy sexuality," but when does one's pursuit of sexual fulfillment become unhealthy, or a *sexual health problem*? It all depends on the consequences of their behavior—that is, it can become a problem when one's *consensual* sexual urges, thoughts, and behaviors lead to he or she acting out sexually despite negative consequences.

Consensual rules out pedophilia, rape, or other sexual violence. *Sexual health problem* rules out mental illnesses such as bipolar disorder, borderline personality disorder, and various antisocial personality disorders.

Having strong sexual interests is not necessarily problematic. Neither is having a lot of sex. Neither is having unusual sexual interests and behaviors as long as nobody gets hurt by them. So, looking at consequences is the only rational way to evaluate how problematic a sexual behavior is. Your partner may not be comfortable with your sexual interests, and the consequence is that this may be causing problems in your relationship. However, there may be nothing inherently unhealthy about your sexual interests. You and your partner may just be incompatible as a couple. Should you modify your sexual interests and behaviors to save your relationship? You cannot change your sexual interests. They are inherent. You can always consider changing your behaviors to save your relationship, but the devil here is in the details. Sometimes changing is possible and worthwhile; sometimes it isn't. Only you can decide.

EROTIC ORIENTATION

I've spoken about the term (or rather, the misnomer) "sexual addiction," which generally refers to sexual behavior that is difficult to stop despite bad consequences. It is possible for a person to be troubled by "out-of-control sexual behaviors" (OCSB), a phrase coined by therapists Douglas Braun-Harvey and Michael Vigorito. I far prefer this term over "sexual addiction." Sometimes, a person's sexual behavior is truly compulsive and difficult to control, despite the consequences. Sometimes, it is "trauma re-enactment" that can be treated by psychotherapy. However, a person can have strong sexual interests he finds difficult to ignore without this being a problem. A person who really likes something may simply want to do it.

Let me be very clear. Some people really like sex. They have a "high sex drive." When should we (or they) decide they are engaging in problematic sexual behavior? Put plainly, wanting or having lots of sex is not a disorder as long as the consequences are not destructive. High-sex-drive people do not necessarily suffer from a psychological problem.

However, we must always consider the issue of consequences. Legal consequences cannot be ignored. In places where sodomy is illegal, couples engaging in anal sex must consider the trouble they might get into, even though anal sex in itself isn't unhealthy. After all, until recently (and in many places still today), being gay was a crime. Social consequences may also be a factor. Being gay is still socially unacceptable in many subcultures of the United States, and being "out" can have consequences, even though there is nothing wrong with being gay. Personal consequences include risk of disease, spending too much money, spending too much time, or otherwise harming yourself without directly harming anyone else. It goes without saying that any behavior that harms others is unhealthy and must be stopped. How long should a person be allowed to put only himself at jeopardy before an intervention is called for? There is no easy answer.

No matter how unusual a sexual fantasy might be, it is not automatically "problematic." Problems are defined by consequences, and only behaviors have consequences. Yes, individuals, society, and the law often define "problematic sex" by type or category, but this is not psychologically justified. Even so, to protect yourself, you should keep in mind that behavior that seems to you to be "obviously innocent" may get you into trouble with your neighbors or the law.

What Is OCSB?

The term OCSB puts the emphasis on what the individual wants, rather than the term "sex addiction," which puts the emphasis on the "sexual behavior" and commits itself to a rigid addiction model that too often is harmful. OCSB focuses on the point of view of a client who comes to see a therapist with concerns that his sexual behavior *feels* "out of control." The therapist then can work conjointly with the client to develop a reasonable plan to make things better. OCSB rejects the idea that treatment is being imposed on the client by an outside "authority," as is the case with "sexual addiction" treatment programs.

OCSB represents a perspective in the therapeutic community to stop being sex-negative, to focus on problems people are actually having, and staying away from moral and religious rules and regulations. Being gay isn't bad; masturbating isn't bad; porn isn't bad; BDSM isn't bad. Calling these behaviors "bad" is essentially a moral judgment, and we therapists want to focus on the practical problems people are having, not moral theories. Perhaps someone is privately engaging in sexual behavior that, for whatever reason, their partner finds disgusting. In other words, "I feel disgusted; therefore, you are disgusting." This is more the problem of the person with the disgust response than that of the person engaging in the behavior. Your sexual behavior is "out of control" only if you decide it is. No one else has the right to decide this for you. Again, getting into trouble around sex doesn't necessarily mean you are at fault. The trouble might be circumstantial, not inherent. It could be grounded in religion, culture, or the tastes of the people around you. Any of these things can create conflict for you, but it doesn't mean there's something wrong with you.

On the other hand, it is common for some people to *think* they have OCSB even when an outside observer might not reach that conclusion. By our definition of OCSB, these people *do* have OCSB, because their sexual behaviors are troubling them. These individuals are often characterized by their *attitude* toward sexuality. They tend to share some of the following characteristics: They are religious, have negative attitudes about porn, are judgmental about (their own and other people's) sexual morality, are more depressed, have substance abuse problems, are more prone to sexual boredom, and/or have naturally high sex drives. I see in my clients with OCSB significant shame, especially sexual shame. They usually have a lack of accurate sex education and commonly fight their natural sexual desires, especially fetishes and kinks.

Realistically, though, if you are constantly putting yourself at risk with your sexual behavior, regret it but can't seem to stop, then you may indeed have a problem. Some therapists say it doesn't matter whether you call it "sex addiction," "OCSB," "problematic sexual behavior," or "compulsive sexual behavior." However, it does matter greatly because what you call it determines how you will treat it! Calling it "sex addiction" pathologizes the behavior rather than understanding what is driving the actual behavior. Getting a differential diagnosis is essential as we already have well-established assessments and diagnoses that explain why someone feels out of control with their sexual behavior.

Here are some of the reasons someone might engage in hypersexual behaviors:

- Bipolar Disorder
- Affect Dysregulation
- Intimacy and Attachment Disorder
- Sexual Abuse/Trauma
- Coming out gay, bisexual or with new sexual fantasies
- High Sex Drive
- Personality Disorder
- Shame
- Kinks/Sexual Fetishisms (Intense Sexual Interests to atypical objects)

And of course, the experience of being and feeling out of control might be because it is normal for them but not for their relationship, religion, or their own personal values. Here, then, the issue is holding a space for someone to experience erotic tension between things they hold dearly and value for themselves and have to work it out.

Generally, it is wise to seek the advice of a therapist who specializes in treating sexual problems; i.e., a certified sex therapist.

The case of Colin

I recently had a client I'll call Colin who came to consult with me about his "sexual addiction." He was ashamed because he enjoyed what he called "compulsive masturbation" and looking at pornography of men with big penises. He had been working with a series of therapists who told him in no uncertain terms that his masturbation was compulsive. They said that he ought to want to express his sexuality in a loving committed relationship. He wasn't in such a relationship (they said) because of his "addiction." His therapists had recommended 12-step groups for sex addicts, and he had dutifully attended these groups.

When I asked him if being in a loving, committed relationship was what he wanted, he responded, "Shouldn't that be what I want?" I replied that he should want whatever *he* wanted. He had a full social life and very close friends. He had a prior partner of 10 years whom he loved, but it didn't work out though they remained friends. He was neither yearning for another partner nor excluding the possibility. I asked him to consider whether masturbation and fantasy *were* actually what he wanted.

Had I been following the strict sex-addiction model, I would have pushed Colin to wonder why he was "avoiding" relationships, and I would have attempted to convince him that his compulsive masturbation was interfering with his life. Like his other therapists I would have directed him to 12-step programs to stop the masturbation, to work on dating and finding himself a partner.

I would have examined his childhood with him for sexual, physical, and emotional abuse. Anything we found would have been explored as possibly contributing to his "addiction." We would have come up with nonsexual ways he could self-soothe himself to make it easier for him to give up masturbation. If Colin had continued to masturbate, in my role as a sex-addiction therapist I would have been forced to conclude that he was "slipping" and "relapsing" and never "recovering" until he stopped.

However, my approach to help Colin was different. I examined with him—from his point of view and values—whether or not *he* felt his sexual behavior was compulsive and interfering in his life. In fact, he told me that he enjoyed what he was doing. He was open to the possibility that someday someone special might come along, but a relationship was not high on his list of needs. He had assumed it should be, because that's what his sex-addiction therapists had told him.

Colin and I did talk about his past to see what parts might be driving how he expressed his sexuality, not assuming we'd find something pathological, but rather just for understanding. Using the perspective of OCSB, even if Colin's masturbation and porn use could have been linked to childhood neglect or abuse, I still would not have labeled his sexual behavior a problem unless he thought it was one himself.

I encouraged him to let go of any shame that he had about how he enjoyed himself. I didn't say he had to be in a relationship. I didn't try to move him in any particular direction. This is very different from my earlier training as a sexual addiction therapist in which I was taught to push the client toward "relational sexual health."

All of us have threads from our childhood that influence our sexual desires, fantasies and behaviors. You have an opportunity to learn to play with your sexuality and claim it as your own rather than fighting it throughout your life.

Confusing fetishes with compulsive sexual behavior

"I keep going back to this same thing over and over again. I try to stop, but I can't stop. I can't control it." This is what might be called a compulsion: An interest or behavior with failed attempts to stop, spending more and more amounts of time engaged with it, wanting it more and more. But this pattern also captures any hobby or profession that becomes more and more engrossing, from watching football to playing video games. Many of the young scientists and engineers I've interviewed have been utterly consumed by their profession, spending almost all their time on it, often neglecting other important things in their lives. But sex is less respectable in our society than science or engineering!

EROTIC ORIENTATION

Expressing your natural sexuality is not necessarily unhealthy, and "trying to stop" something so fundamental to your nature is bound to fail. As the late psychologist Jack Morin famously summarized, "If you go to war with your sexuality, you will lose and end up in more trouble than before you started." Fetishes can feel especially like compulsions, their pull is so strong. But most fetishes are harmless. The harm comes from fighting your own sexual nature. If you are at odds with your sexuality, fighting it will contribute to your grief around it.

For instance, as I briefly discussed in Chapter 8, spanking turns some people on. But you may be turned on by spanking and spending too much time and money on your computer with spanking porn. The problem is not the fact that you are turned on by spanking, which you cannot change. The problem is the time and money that you need to manage more effectively. If you are struggling with a psychological compulsion—perhaps you are re-enacting childhood trauma—then you may need therapy to give you control over the compulsion. But being turned on by spanking is inherent to your sexuality. When you have successfully completed therapy and can now manage your time and money, spanking will still turn you on. This remains true even if you never look at porn again. A celibate priest is still a sexual person, merely one who has chosen to not act with respect to his sexuality (or has acted in contravention to his vows, as recent revelations about sexual abuse in the church have shown).

Some "authorities" and leaders of the sexual addiction community have an extreme overreaction to fetishes. In response to the mildest forms of BDSM play they say things like "All violence is bad and must be stopped." I take the position that nonstandard sexual tastes are not necessarily bad. Men are especially likely to have fetishes (twenty times more likely than women, in fact). How you're wired, what you're into may be nonstandard but it's not necessarily "bad."

Childhood sexual abuse

Studies have estimated that one in four women have been sexually abused, and one in six boys have been sexually abused. What is the nature of childhood sexual abuse? Abuse occurs when an adult dominates and exploits a child—thereby violating trust and the promise of protection. Abuse can occur in any relationship with a power differential. The abuser uses his superior position to manipulate, misuse, degrade, humiliate, or even hurt another—who, by inference, is always inferior. Many studies have confirmed that the basic motivation for rape is power, not sex. Other forms of sexual abuse follow the same pathology.

The sexual abuser's ideal target is a child who's still naive, lacking the "immune system" imparted by emotional and intellectual experience that tells him when he's being violated—and when to resist, and when to say no. A dominant perpetrator—uncle, stepfather, priest, or other male figure who's familiar, trusted, and seems all-powerful—can easily lure a boy into a sexual relationship and force him to comply.

There are several important points to make about the consequences of childhood sexual abuse.

First, childhood sexual abuse can be a significant trauma that a person carries as a heavy burden into adulthood. An abused person may have a compulsion to act out sexual scripts that reflect the abuse, even if he has "forgotten" that he was abused. This unconscious process is sometimes summarized as "turning trauma into orgasm." Until the source of the trauma is resolved, the sexual re-enactments never end. In other words, unresolved childhood sexual abuse can lead to compulsive sexual behaviors. The adult abused as a child often requires psychotherapy to break the control that the compulsion has over his life.

Second, when a man abuses a boy who is straight, the boy sometimes grows up to feel a compulsion to have sex with men even though he is not gay or bisexual. I discuss this situation at length in my book *Is My Husband Gay, Straight, or Bi?* When the trauma of the abuse is resolved in therapy, the straight man is no longer drawn to sex with men. He was not gay or bisexual. Being abused cannot change a straight boy's orientation, but when the straight man is drawn to want sex with men, he is often confused and thinks he may be gay or bi. I say: Sexual abuse can disorient you, but it cannot orient you.

Third, a boy who *is* gay may be damaged by abuse. When the abused boy grows up, the gay man must deal both with the trauma-induced compulsion to act out sexually with men and also his own gay sexual nature. This confusion can significantly prolong his coming-out process.

Therapy is generally required to resolve the trauma of sexual abuse, whether the man is gay, bi, or straight. Many men who come to my office with problematic sexual behavior learn that the origin of their compulsion is in childhood sexual abuse. Whether he is gay, bi, or straight, the man has been damaged by the trauma of the abuse, but his inherent orientation has not been changed by it. Gay men are taught early on not to be intimate with each other, let alone be open to our families or classmates. Abuse that begins early in a gay boy's life leaves him extremely susceptible to intimacy issues.

Sexual abuse can shape your fantasies, but that's not necessarily something you have to change. A client of mine suffered sexual abuse when he was a child, perpetrated by his best friend's father. The man was significantly hairy, and as a direct result of the abuse, my client was into hairy guys. And that's okay. Yes, the father of his best friend should never have abused him, and there were negative consequences that my client had to deal with in therapy. But being into hairy guys was not one of the consequences that needed to be changed.

One final point: There's a body of published research that shows "abused" and "traumatized" don't always go together. Not everyone who has been sexually abused is traumatized by the abuse. I'm not saying, of course, that abuse is a good thing, only that people differ in the damage they experience from potentially traumatic events. Abuse might affect your sexual taste and at the same time not drive your behavior. But taste doesn't require therapy; only behavior does.

Some gay men who were sexually abused in childhood have told me, "This was my first sexual experience, and I enjoyed it." Early in my career I was very surprised and in disbelief by this. I spent many years confronting my gay clients when they said this. I insisted that they couldn't have enjoyed it, because it was all bad and all abuse. Over time, I've learned from my clients and my training that there are parts of childhood sexual abuse that people sometimes enjoy, and I cannot take that away from them. So, I've moderated my response to my clients who say this, and I'm telling you, my reader, because I want you not to feel ashamed if you reflect back on your childhood sexual abuse and say, "You know, there were parts of it I liked." That's normal. It's okay. It makes sense. It doesn't mean that you liked the abuse. It means that parts of the abuse were your first sexual experience.

OCSB is complex

Behavior can be a problem even if it isn't unhealthy. You must be aware of societal and legal consequences, as well as consequences to yourself and the people you love. If you find yourself endangering yourself, spending too much time and money on sex and porn, engaging in damaging activities and unable to stop in spite of the consequences, then you may need help to address what you are doing and regain control over your behaviors. Be aware that compulsions often have a psychological basis; a good therapist can help you discover what's going on.

But having strong sexual interests is not necessarily unhealthy, not necessarily problematic, not necessarily

EROTIC ORIENTATION

compulsive. Decide if you have a problem by the consequences of your behavior, not by the content of your fantasies. Get help if you need it. Otherwise, enjoy!

A man who was abused as a child can be strongly affected by that experience. He may find his life ruled by sexual compulsions. He may be significantly confused about his orientation. But don't forget that sexual abuse disorients you; it *does not* orient you. This is my most important point. When you deal with the trauma of the abuse, the confusion, the "disorientation" is lifted, and you can discover your true erotic orientation. Your sexual preferences may be permanently affected by the abuse, but through therapy you can still regain control over your sexual behavior, even if that's been a problem.

CONCLUSION

I have touched on only a few of the issues that can be explored in the realm of sex and couples' therapy. There are many more, including how power, control and humiliation can be eroticized, various fetishes, cuckolding, and hotwifing, swinger parties, adult dating apps, and so on. The value of this kind of therapy is to help you discover and understand of your deepest desires around your sexuality, and to help you incorporate healthy sexual practices that can lead to a more fulfilling life. Most importantly, therapy can help you remove unnecessary guilt and shame you have around your sexual and erotic lives.

When couples come into therapy there needs to be two conversations: the relationship and the sexual conversation. Most couple's therapists focus only on the relationship and believe that when the relationship is better, sex will be better. This is not necessarily the case and most often untrue. A sexual-health dialogue needs to occur in addition to other issues in therapy.

Sex is a dangerous and uncomfortable topic. It can threaten one's self-esteem, relationships and even one's relationship to religion, but these will thrive once you discover and accept your own sexual and erotic orientation. It is our birthright to have access to this core part of who we are. Sexual health is a key component of a good life with or without a partner.

I hope this book has given you a start on your road to sexual health.

Made in United States
Orlando, FL
07 July 2024